# GOLD PAVILION

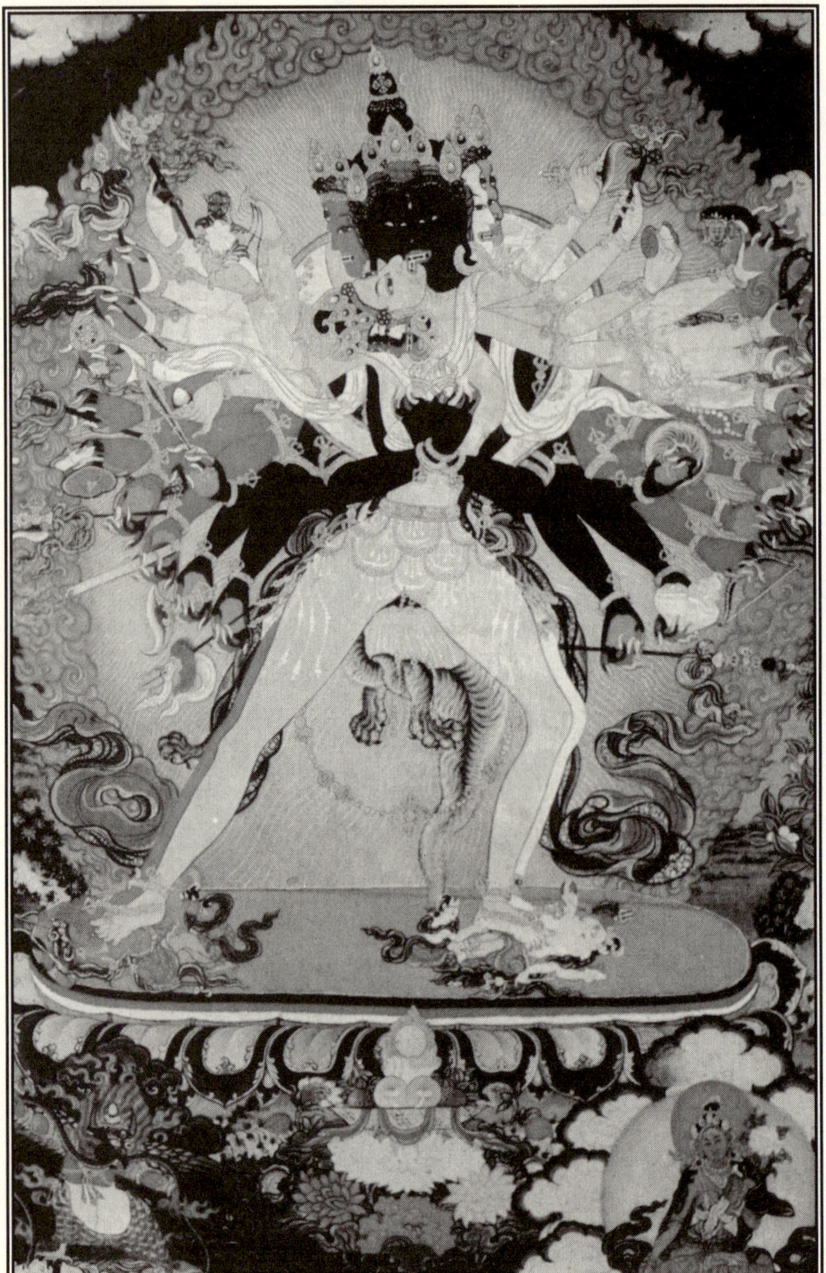

# THE GOLD PAVILION

*Taoist Ways to Peace,
Healing, and Long Life*

MICHAEL SASO

Charles E. Tuttle Co., Inc.
Boston • Rutland, Vermont • Tokyo

First published in 1995 by Charles E. Tuttle Co., Inc.
of Rutland, Vermont and Tokyo, Japan, with editorial offices at
153 Milk Street, Boston, Massachusetts, 02109

© 1995 Michael Saso

All rights reserved.
No part of this publication may be reproduced or utilized in any form or
by any means, electronic or mechanical, including photocopying, recording,
or by any information storage and retrieval system, without prior written
permission from Charles E. Tuttle Co., Inc.

Library of Congress Cataloging-in-Publication Data

Saso, Michael R.
    The Gold Pavilion : Taoist ways to peace, healing, and long life / by Michael Saso.
       p. cm.
    Includes bibliographical references.
    ISBN 0-8048-3060-6
    1.Meditation—Taoism. 2. Healing. 3. Longevity. I. Huang t'ing ching. English. II. Title.
BL1923.S27  1995
299'.51443—dc20                                                  95-24661
                                                                            CIP

First Edition
1  3  5  7  9  10  8  6  4  2    04  03  02  01  00  99  98  97  96  95

Frontispiece: *Kalachakra. The male image, Mahakala, stands for compassion, the female, wisdom (see chapter 5). Mongol tanka, 16th century.*

Book design by Jill Winitzer
Cover design by Sherry Fatla
Printed in the United States of America

*To my mother, Beatrice Saso, who wonders what I do in the hills of China and Tibet, and to the monks, nomads, and others who made the sojourning so eventful. To the late Zhuang Chen Dengyun, who taught the meditations of the* Yellow Court Canon *as interpreted in these pages; the lay Taoists, men and women, of the Yuanxuanxue Yuan in Samdiptam, Kowloon, who practice Taoist meditation in their daily lives; and the Taoist master Shi Daochang, who learned these practices before the Japanese burning of Mao Shan in 1938 and the Red Guard destruction of the sacred mountain between 1966 and 1978 and taught "quieting the heart" (*ding xin*) until his death on Mao Shan in 1989.*

# Contents

*Preface ix*

CHAPTER ONE
*A Brief Introduction to Taoist Meditation 1*

CHAPTER TWO
*Interior Peace 27*

CHAPTER THREE
*Centering Meditation; Colors that Heal 71*

CHAPTER FOUR
*The Gold Pavilion Classic: Taoist Emptying Meditation 99*

CHAPTER FIVE
*Tantric Meditation 153*

*Notes 169*

APPENDIX
*A Comparative Chart of Taoist History 183*

*Glossary and Index of Special Terms 185*

*Bibliography and Further Readings 203*

# Preface

The *Gold Pavilion: Taoist Ways to Peace, Health, and Long Life* is a step-by-step description of a way of Taoist meditation from ancient China. The first proponent of this form of meditation was a woman named Wei Huacun (Wei Hua-ts'un), who lived in the fourth century (d. ca. 330 C.E.). Married, with two sons who were employed at the court in Nanjing (Nan-ching, then called Jinling, "Gold Hill"), she received a Taoist ordination and practiced meditation on or near the sacred Taoist mountain called Mao Shan. Her methods of meditation, which called for the emptying of the mind of all negative judgments and the heart of selfish desires, were the foundation of a special kind of Taoism called the Highest Pure school, founded atop Mao Shan (see map). Inner peace and healing were the results of her meditation. *The Huang-t'ing Ching*, the *Gold Pavilion* classic, is the text of the meditation attributed to her. The Chinese title literally means "Yellow Pavilion," if translated in the standard dictionary meaning. The color to be visualized with this meditation in the

*The Gold Pavilion*

Taoist tradition is a bright gold-yellow. The proper translation of the term, therefore, is "Gold Pavilion."

This book proposes a way to find inner peace and wholeness in a world with little time for quiet contemplation. I am indebted to many Taoists, laymen and -women as well as ordained priests, who explained so patiently the meaning of the *Gold Pavilion* classic. I am especially grateful to Zhao Zhendong (Chao Chen-tung), director of the Yuanxuanxue Yuan Taoist complex in Samdiptam, New Territories, Kowloon, who provided the written manuals, i.e., prompt books, used in the annotations of chapter 4. The Taoist master Min Zhiting (Min Chih-t'ing) of White Cloud Temple, Beijing; the late Shi Daochang (Shih Tao-ch'ang) of Mao Shan near Nanjing; and Zhuang Jiaxin (Chuang Chia-hsin) of Xinzhu (Hsinchu), Taiwan, explained their own meditative and ritual use of the *Gold Pavilion* text. To these and many others, I express my thanks.

Though the text of the *Gold Pavilion* classic is written in metaphor and symbol, the method of meditation is in fact simple and easy. The quelling first of negative judgment, and then of all judgment (the joining of a verb to a noun) is a meditative prelude to a life of inner peace and well-being. The person who learns to meditate as described in these pages finds peace and long life and brings healing to others.

The *Gold Pavilion* classic, in the interpretation of traditional Taoist masters, teaches the method of emptying prayer in a manner that even the layperson and nonexpert can follow. The reader is introduced to the meditation in chapters 2 and 3. An interpretation of the *Gold Pavilion* classic is given in chapter 4. I compare Tibetan Tantric meditation and other forms of

*Preface*

apophatic or emptying prayer with Taoist practices in chapter 5. The total body (i.e., Tantric) style of prayer described here is used today in many parts of Tibet and modern mainland and overseas China.

That is to say, the meditations taught in the Taoist *Gold Pavilion* classic are similar to a genre of prayer techniques shared by many religious traditions. All of these traditions teach the use of body, mouth, and mind together in union when praying. In Buddhism this kind of total body prayer is called Tantric meditation. It is usually learned orally from a master, rather than from a book. Just as we must learn to swim, drive a car, or fly an airplane by taking lessons and then actually swimming, driving, or flying, so too Taoist Tantric prayer must be learned by "jumping in" to practice.

Masters of Taoist prayer sometimes do write out the directions for Tantric meditation in an easy-to-follow fashion. The commentary used to translate the *Gold Pavilion* classic is such a text. It helps understand the cryptic text itself. It contains directions for doing Tantric meditation without recourse to a living master. In such a case, the text is the master, whose words of explanation were once written down by an unknown disciple so as not to forget the master's instructions.

The oral directions that the master adds to the text and commentary are in fact descriptions of spiritual forces unleashed or controlled by the person doing the meditations. The illustrations found throughout the book show what these spiritual forces look like in the teachings of Tibetan and Taoist masters. When a text calls for a color, as for instance the blue-green color of new leaves in spring, the master describes what the blue-green spirit of spring looks like. For the Taoist it is in fact the personified spirit of the East, a bearded ancient called Fu Xi (Fu Hsi), patron of the family and the element wood. For the Tantric Buddhist he is Dhrtarastra, in the Judeo-Christian tradition, Gabriel; each religious tradition has set images depicted in art and envisioned in contemplative meditation.

Taoist, biblical, and Tantric symbols sometimes juxtapose male and female images, seen embracing in close physical union. The Canticle of Canticles in the Bible, the Tibetan tanka pictures, and some passages of the *Gold Pavilion* classic are examples of such images. There are at least three possible interpretations of these stunningly graphic symbols. The first is literal (that is, they depict sexual union). The second is figurative: the male represents compassion and the female wisdom (compassion is tempered by wisdom). The third, truly Taoist or Tantric, meaning is that all visions, good or bad, are relative and must be burned away by the fires and washed clean by the waters of Tantric meditation. The *Gold Pavilion* classic embraces this last interpretation.

In the true Taoist and Tantric traditions, the spiritual forces unleashed by prayer, whether good or bad, must be emptied from the mind and heart before union with the unmoving transcendent "other shore" can be realized. Tantric and Taoist prayer are therefore basically techniques for emptying the mind of images and the heart of desires, preludes to "being one with the Tao," or one with the "other shore" of wisdom. The meditations that bring about this state of emptiness (called kenosis in Western religious traditions) also bring great peace, health, and serenity, preludes to an encounter with the absolute.

# Preface

The Chinese words used in this book are generally romanized first in modern pinyin, which is the preferred system of the People's Republic of China, and then using the Wade-Giles system (usually in parentheses). The exceptions to this are the words in chapter 4 and ancient names and titles that are already familiar in their Wade-Giles transliterations (i.e., Chuang-tzu, *Tao-te Ching*).

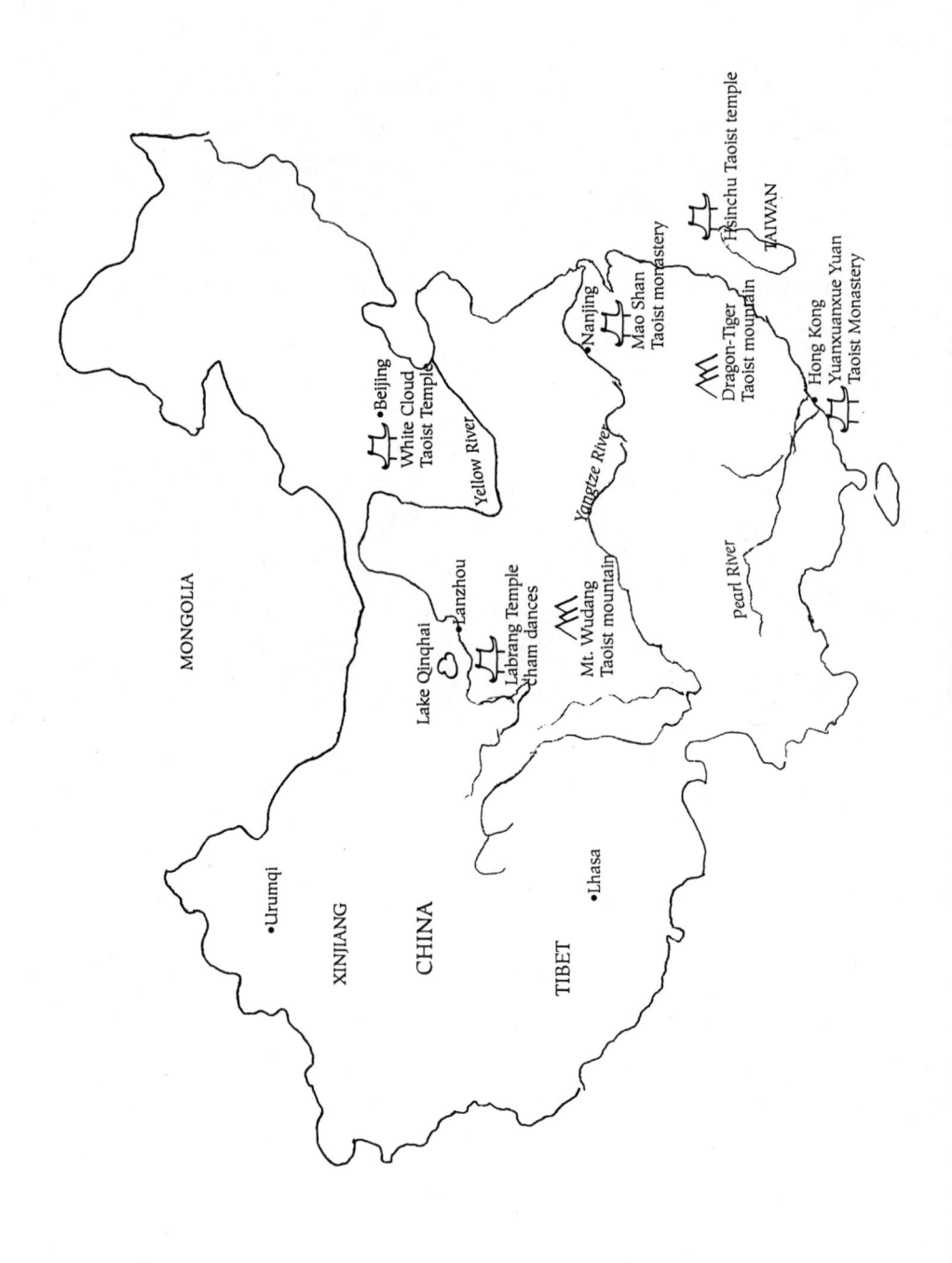

❈ Chapter One

# A Brief Introduction to Taoist Meditation

Taoism (the *T* is pronounced like a *D*) is one of China's three great philosophical systems. With Confucianism and Buddhism it gives enduring value to Chinese culture. Confucianism provides guidelines for perceptive human relations. Buddhism teaches a sense of compassion for the living and care for the afterlife. Taoism furthers a sense of well-being and harmony with nature that fosters long life and good health. The popular saying *sanjiao gui yi*, "the Three Teachings make a whole person," suggests the idea that we are somehow better, more complete human beings by learning from all three systems. The person who is filled with respect and benevolence for others and compassion for all living things, and who lives in close harmony with nature, lives long and is filled with inner peace and blessing.

Another popular saying states: "Confucianism for the head, Buddhism for the heart, and Taoism for the belly." The Confucian tradition advocates the rational side of human life. Buddhism teaches kindness of heart toward the living and the chanting of sutras to alleviate sorrow for the deceased. Taoism offers ways to bring health, interior peace, and long life by harmonizing the human body with change in the outer world of nature. By integrating philosophy, meditation, diet, and exercise, Taoism reputedly can heal illness and slow the aging process.

Many Asian and Western scholars divide Taoism into two portions, a philosophy for savants and a religion for satisfying the ritual needs of unenlightened peasants. Popular Taoism, they point out, heals by exorcism, celebrates village festivals, and uses alchemy (chemical medicines that can harm when taken as an overdose; in this sense, Western medicine too is a kind of sophisticated alchemy) to prolong life.

Taoists themselves do not make such distinctions. Taoism is simply a way of maintaining inner peace and harmony. To be healthy, one's personal philosophy, religion, medication, and eating habits must be in tune with one another. Physical exercise, meditation (also called internal alchemy), good eating habits, festive holidays, good thoughts and actions, are required for a whole and healthy life. Taoism considers all these as a single process leading to peace, long life, and happiness.

In its original sense, the English word *healing* means in fact "to be whole." The word *curing*, on the other hand, means to use a chemical on the skin of a dead animal to make it into leather. Thus the term *Taoist healing* is more appropriate than *Taoist curing*. The Taoist ideal is to heal illness by making the entire person whole, rather than to cure a part of the body without healing the entire person of illness. True healing means making the whole person well.

# A Brief Introduction to Taoist Meditation

Common sense dictates that we listen to our doctor when he or she prescribes Western medicine. Sometimes Western medicines cure one part of the body but harm other parts. Chemotherapy destroys cancer cells but causes harm to many other organs while doing so. Steroids such as prednisone, even simple remedies such as aspirin, can cause internal bleeding and harm the immune system if taken too long or in large dosages. The Taoist ideal is to be positive, happy, and peaceful when taking these medicines so that they work quickly, before too much harm is done to other parts of the body. The Taoist master encourages the patient to obey the doctor, take the medicine prescribed, undergo the operation, and recover quickly by healing (making whole) all the other parts of life as well.

Taoism is a perennial system of healing meditation that has been in practice from ancient times until the present day. The Taoist "way that never parted" draws on many sources:

- The *I Ching* shows how to act in accord with nature's changes.
- The *Tao-te Ching* teaches how to find and follow the Tao.
- The *Chuang-tzu* tells how to empty the mind and heart of all negative thoughts and judgments and live with good humor in order to find the Tao.
- Yin-yang five phase philosophy attunes humans to nature's changes.
- The *Gold Pavilion* classic finds Tao within, by emptying the mind and heart of all concepts, even sacred spiritual images.

## The Gold Pavilion

More than three thousand years have elapsed since the earliest phrases of the *I Ching* (pinyin *Yijing*, Book of Changes) were formulated about 1100 B.C.E.[1] The basic books for all Taoists, Lao-tzu's *Tao-te Ching* (pinyin *Laozi Daode Jing*, Classic for Attaining the Tao) and the *Chuang-tzu* (pinyin *Zhuangzi*) were composed in the fourth century B.C.E.[2] The yin-yang five phase system (*yinyang wuxing*), explained in chapter 3, evolved during and after this period. Based on all of these sources, Taoists elaborated a plan of village festivals, healing, and burials from the second century onward. Like many streams feeding into a mighty river, alchemy, meditation, mountain ascetics and hermits, healing methods, physical exercises, martial arts, and breathing exercises, all became identified with Taoism during this lengthy period of time.

During the Ming and Qing dynasties (mid-fourteenth to early twentieth centuries) Taoism fell out of favor at court. Scholars considered all later developments to be aberrations from the original purity of Lao-tzu and Chuang-tzu's works.[3] Followers of the sixth to the fourth century B.C.E. texts were called Daojia (Tao-chia), "school Taoists." Later movements were named Daojiao (Tao-chiao), "ritual" or "festive" Taoism. Festive healing Taoism was called superstitious, a "parting of the way," thus indicating that Taoism had in fact two paths, a higher pure philosophy for the learned and a lower form of superstitious rites for the peasant.

Taoists do not recognize these distinctions. For the followers of Lao-tzu, the very use of distinction and thought-splitting is itself a form of illness. In chapter 71 of the *Tao-te Ching* the separation of knowledge and philosophy from reality is said to cause sickness. In the opening chapters of the *Chuang-tzu*

# A Brief Introduction to Taoist Meditation

the judging of "good and bad," "high and low," separates one from the Tao. The Taoist tradition finds wholeness essential for well-being. Only when philosophy, ritual, festival, and human living are in harmony can healing take place, and Taoists who follow this way are noted for their long lives.

## Special Taoist Terms

There are a number of technical words used by Taoists when teaching and practicing the method of healing meditation. These concepts bear a special Taoist meaning. The first such term is *ritual*, a word that people of Western culture do not like to hear or talk about.[4] For most it means an outmoded, stilted form of behavior reserved for old-fashioned church services, which are best avoided. Ritual does not have this connotation in the Taoist system. Rather, rituals are actions that derive from the animal or physical part of us. Rites are by nature repetitious, meant to be performed again and again on special occasions. Eating, bathing, all bodily functions are ritual actions. Christmas, Thanksgiving, Hanukkah, Valentine's Day, the Fourth of July, are all ritual occasions that elicit actions repeated annually that satisfy basic physical needs within us. The mating of birds, the making of a bed, cleaning a room, walking the dog at the beach, dancing a waltz or a tango, even disco dancing, are rituals. Without ritual, life would have no celebrations.

Healing, too, is a ritual. In the healing process certain acts are prescribed to heal certain forms of illness. These acts include not only taking the medicine but also observing the directions on the bottle. Some medicines are taken before, and some after, meals. Some are taken with water, others with food. Taoist healing prescribes quiet meditation, happy thoughts, and good eating and breathing habits as a part of healing ritual. The word ritual therefore does not have a negative connotation in the Taoist system.

The second term that must be understood before talking about Taoism is *spirit*. There are many Chinese words translated by the single English word spirit.[5] These include the notion that the human soul continues to exist after death, and that unseen powers of nature operate in an invisible spiritual order.

Long ago the Chinese personified the forces of nature by giving them spiritual names and ascribing specific powers to them. These spiritual forces of nature ruled like the feudal lords of ancient China. The Taoist's ritual meditation "exorcises," that is, rids the mind of fear by expelling such "demons," whether seen to be ancestors or some unknown power in nature. Relieving religious fear is an essential part of healing.

It is not surprising to learn that in general the Taoist does not fear spirits.[6] The Taoist learns how to conceptualize (imagine) lists of spirits and exorcise them from his or her own consciousness, as well as from the mind of a sick person. The *Gold Pavilion* classic (*Huang-t'ing Ching*), one of the basic meditations taught by the great fourth-century Taoist mystic Lady Wei Huacun (Wei Hua-ts'un), rids the consciousness of all spiritual images before one meditates on the transcendent Tao.[7]

Following the ideas of this fourth-century Taoist, most modern Taoists use very dramatic methods to drive the fear of spirits and demons out of the minds of those who are to be healed. Visualizing and then exorcising or "emptying out" the mind of all spiritual images, even if an image is good or if the

# A Brief Introduction to Taoist Meditation

spirit is thought to exist only in the mind, is very much a part of Taoist and also of Tibetan Tantric Buddhist practice. The similarity between Taoist and Tibetan Buddhist emptying prayer is described in chapter 5.

Another concept that must be understood before entering into the subject of healing is the definition of a Taoist. The term *Taoist, daoshi,* pronounced "daoshr" in Chinese, means a man or woman who has been ordained or set aside and specially trained to perform a specific role in society. Anyone can learn about Taoist healing, but only those who have been trained and initiated in the Taoist tradition are truly "Taoists."

In order to be a recognized Taoist, one must fulfill three requirements: one must find and be accepted and trained by a licensed Taoist master (men and women are considered equal in the Taoist tradition); one must learn to meditate on the writings of Lao-tzu and Chuang-tzu, and promise to obey the rules and learn to play the music, sing the songs, and dance the steps of Taoist ritual; and one must receive a Taoist "register" (*lu*) or list of spirits to be envisioned, talismans to summon them, and mantra to command them, that is, empty them from the heart and mind before meditating on the Tao.[8] It is not necessary to be a Taoist to learn Taoist prayer and healing, but by the same token one should not boast of being a Taoist simply because one has learned something about healing, ritual, meditation, or other practices. Though many experts in China and elsewhere claim to be Taoist, and though they may be excellent teachers of breathing, meditation, healing, or *qi* (*ch'i*) exercise, only those men and women who have fulfilled the three conditions outlined above are really ordained Taoists. It is the sign of a true Taoist master to claim to know nothing, to remain hidden, to avoid praise and fame, and to take no monetary recompense for healing.

## Identifying Taoists by Ritual and Color

Having defined what a Taoist is from within the Taoist tradition, we must now try to identify what is and what is not Taoist from the many practices found throughout China, Taiwan, Hong Kong, and elsewhere in Asia. There are certain kinds of healing rites that are not really Taoist, though their practitioners may claim them to be. There are other practices, such as "sexual hygiene" (*fangzhong*), descriptions of which sell very well in American book markets, that are outside the Taoist tradition and forbidden to the true Taoist to practice or countenance.[9]

Throughout most of southeast China and Taiwan, Taoists are classified into two kinds, "Redhat" (*hungtou*) and "Blackhat" (*wutou*). The meaning of this color symbol differs from place to place in China. In most of southern Taiwan Redhat popular Taoists wrap a red cloth around their heads during ritual, and perform exorcisms and healing only for the living. Blackhat classical Taoists perform burial ritual for the dead, healing, and the Jiao festival of village renewal for the living.

In northern Taiwan, however, a far more complicated system exists. Throughout this entire area, Redhat Taoists use the same ritual vestments as Blackhats, a black hat with a gold crown, and perform more or less the same rites of renewal (*jiao*) in the village temple. A momentous difference lies in the fact that the Blackhat Taoists actually "empty out" all the spirits from the

## A Brief Introduction to Taoist Meditation

temple and their own body, while the Redhats summon the spirits into the temple for a feast. During the Redhat rituals the prayers of the village are simply offered up to the visiting spirits in the hope that the requests of the villagers will be granted.

In addition to the fact that the Redhats do not empty themselves of spirits during prayer but rather fill the mind and the temple with the benign spirits' presence, there is another important difference: the people do not call the Redhat priests Taoists or daoshi but rather *fashi* or *sigong* (Fujian dialect: *hoatsu, saigong*), that is, ritual masters rather than Taoist masters.

This notion of filling rather than emptying indicates that the Redhat practices may once have derived from the medium or shaman traditions, not the Taoist. The medium is a trance expert who when possessed by a spirit can talk in tongues and sometimes heal. A shaman is a ritual expert who when in a trance can travel to another spiritual realm to look into the well-being of the deceased, heal the living, and bring the prayers of the villagers to the heavenly spirits. Both the medium and the shaman are unconscious of their acts when in trance. The Redhat priests act as interpreters for the mediums and sometimes become mediums themselves. The color red symbolizes filling rather than emptying for the majority of Redhat fashi.

To test this hypothesis (Redhats practice kataphatic prayer; Blackhats apophatic), I traveled throughout southern Fujian and northern Gwangdong Provinces, looking for Taoists and their registers. There is in fact a Redhat Taoist in Zhangzhou city, in southeast Fujian, who had received a bona fide *lu* register, knew the meditations of emptying, and had a classic Taoist license. The terms Redhat and Blackhat are therefore relative to the place where they are used. The reason the

*The Taoist envisions the five colors, five directions, as spirits from the five internal organs and sends out all spirit-images before meditating on the Tao. Ch'ing dynasty woodblock print from* Xingming Guizhi.

# A Brief Introduction to Taoist Meditation

definition of *red* and *black* varies is that any person (including the reader) may go to one of the sacred Taoist mountains in China, find a master, study the registers, and receive a Taoist license. The Taoist tradition, whether using the term *red* or *black*, is truly Taoist (as defined in this book) only if it empties the mind of spirits and their images.[10]

It is interesting to note that medium, shaman, and priest all practice healing. The medium, the shaman, and the popular fashi Redhat heal by visualization, while the Taoist daoshi heals by kenosis, by emptying the mind and heart of all spirits and their images. It is important that healing takes place, no matter which method is used. The purpose of this work is not to disparage those systems using visualization but to explain the process of Taoist "kenotic" healing, the emptying of worries from the mind and unfulfilled desires from the heart. My study "Mystic, Shaman, Oracle, Priest" delves further into these distinctions than I will here.[11]

From the above discussion it can be seen that at least two kinds of healers, and therefore two different philosophies of well-being (among many others), can be found in Asia. The first kind, which we are describing here, can be called the apophatic or kenotic tradition, which in simple language means emptying the mind of concept and image. The second is the kataphatic or "imaging" tradition, which heals by filling the mind with thoughts of good spirits and well-being.

The kataphatic tradition, using medium possession or shaman trance to heal, can be very dramatic and even traumatic. The possessed mediums sometimes cut themselves with knives, blow on trumpets, and act out the terrifying battle between the forces of good and evil. The medium or shaman is impervious to the attack of evil, can draw a sharp knife across the tongue, dance on sharp blades, or walk on fire without harm to the body. The symbolic drama of the medium and shaman prove the efficacy of exorcism in the healing process. Such practices differ substantially from the healing practices of the apophatic "emptying" Taoist.

The apophatic or emptying tradition of Taoism uses images to heal. Colors, sound (music), taste, smell, touch, and physical motion are important elements in human well-being. Images are envisioned and "good" thoughts elicited in the mind of the patient. But in the end, all thoughts, images, sounds, and colors are sublimated and emptied out in the encounter with the transcendent Tao, (*wuwei zhi dao*), the source of life, breath, and well-being. Healing, wholeness, and oneness with nature's processes are one and the same experience. Arriving at this experience of oneness through the Tao's transcendent "nonimage" process is the goal of Taoist meditation and a vital element of Taoist healing. Color meditation and imaging are taught in chapter 3, and the prayer of apophasis is described in chapter 4. Men and women who practice these meditations and follow the other directives of the Taoist way of life for the most part live to a happy and healthy old age, climb the high mountains, and celebrate festivals for the villages of China.

## An Outline of Taoist History

After one learns some of the methods of Taoist meditation and healing, the appetite is awakened to understand something about Taoism and its lengthy history in China. Taoism is like a

# A Brief Introduction to Taoist Meditation

great river that flows throughout the entire concourse of Chinese history. Like the Yellow and the Yangtze Rivers, it is fed by many tributaries. Some of these tributaries contain muddy waters. Others do not flow into the mainstream of Taoism but follow their own independent course. Taoism itself blends quietly into the flow of Chinese history, often going unnoticed by official Chinese historians.

The history of China is divided into twenty-four dynasties. Each dynasty was begun by a soldier-emperor who conquered China by the sword. Any given dynasty's history was later rewritten by literate Confucian scholars who often sought to please the reigning emperor rather than the fallen dynasty. Historians are famous for putting Buddhists, Taoists, women, and non-Han Chinese minorities last, after selectively describing the past dynasty's emperors, family, wars, intrigues at court, and other details that pleased the Confucian mind. Thus most dynastic histories do not say good things about Taoists, minorities, Buddhists, or other non-Confucian topics.

Taoism's development within the dynastic records is as follows:

### ● PREDYNASTY MYTHS
*the Five Emperors, before recorded history*
- Fu Hsi (Fu Xi), emperor of the east, founder of the home and the family
- Shen Nung (Shen Nong), emperor of the south, farming and fertility
- Huang Ti (Huangdi), emperor of the center, silk weaving and medicine

*The Gold Pavilion*

⊛

    Shao Hao (Shaohao), emperor of the west, burial and
        afterlife rites
    Chüan Hsü (Zhuanxu), emperor of the north, martial arts
        and exorcism
  **the Three Rulers**: gray cord-marked pottery era
    Yao, heaven-appointed ruler because of human virtue
    Shun, appointed Yao's successor because of virtue
    Yü the Great, who controlled the floods; Xia dynasty
        founded

⊛ THE SHANG-YIN DYNASTY, 1760–1100 B.C.E.: oracle bones, bronze, jade culture

⊛ THE ZHOU DYNASTY, 1100–221 B.C.E. DIVIDED INTO:
  *the Golden Era, to 771 B.C.E.*
  *the Spring-Autumn period, 771–481 B.C.E.*: Lao-tzu, Confucius, many kingdoms
  *the Warring States period, 481–221 B.C.E.*: various philosophical schools

⊛ THE QIN DYNASTY, 221–207 B.C.E.: building of the Great Wall is begun

⊛ THE HAN DYNASTY, 206 B.C.E.–220 C.E.: Confucian exam system; first Buddhist monks in China; Dragon-Tiger Zhengyi religious Taoism founded

⊛ THE THREE KINGDOMS PERIOD, 221–265: Taoist religion approved by the Wei State

⊛ THE PERIOD OF DIVISION, 265–589: the growth of Buddhism and Taoism; Taoist ritual and Lady Wei Huacun's meditation system developed
  *the Western Jin dynasty, 265–316*
  *the North, West, and East Wei dynasties, 386–550;* Buddhism favored

# A Brief Introduction to Taoist Meditation

*the North Ch'i dynasty, 550–557*

*the North Zhou dynasty, 557–589:* Taoist scripture *Wushang Biyao*[12] catalogues various kinds of Taoist ritual meditation.

*the Liu-Sung dynasty, 420–502:* Taoist canonical scriptures catalogued

*the Liang dynasty, 502–557:* Buddhism and Taoism favored

- THE SUI DYNASTY, 589–618: China reunified
- THE TANG DYNASTY, 619–906: height of medieval Chinese civilization; Taoist texts are included in civil service examinations; Tantric Buddhism in China and Tibet
- THE PERIOD OF FIVE KINGDOMS: LATE LIANG, 907; LATE TANG, 923; LATE JIN, 936; LATE HAN, 947; LATE CHOU, 951
- THE SUNG (SONG) DYNASTY: religious reformation in China

  *the Northern Song, 960–1126:* Taoism favored at court

  *the Southern Song, 1127–1281:* Dragon-Tiger Taoism favored

- THE YÜAN (MONGOL) DYNASTY, 1281–1368: Quanzhen Taoism flourishes. Tantric Buddhism flourishes in Tibet.
- THE MING (CHINESE) DYNASTY, 1368–1644: Taoism less favored at court; Mongolia accepts Tibetan Tantric Buddhism.
- THE CH'ING (MANCHU) DYNASTY, 1644–1912: Taoism out of favor; foreign colonial interests in China support Christian missions
- REPUBLIC OF CHINA, 1912–1949: devastating war with Japan, without reparation

- **THE PEOPLE'S REPUBLIC OF CHINA, 1949–PRESENT:**
  Marxist-socialism in China
  *1949–1967:* collectives, communes, suppression of religion
  *1967–1978:* the Great Cultural Revolution, social and economic ruin
  *1979–present:* economic reform, market economy, state capitalism, "socialism with Chinese characteristics," controlled practice of religion

The above outline does not indicate the development of Taoist meditation or the liturgical system that accompanied its growth as a popular movement. The following outline indicates the development of Taoist contemplative prayer.

## Taoist Meditation

The history of Taoist meditation in China can be summarized as follows:

- The two great Taoist thinkers Lao-tzu and Chuang-tzu lived between the sixth and fourth centuries B.C.E. Their works, based on the principle of emptying and nonjudgmental thinking, are the philosophical roots of all subsequent Taoist practices.

- Religious Taoism combined Lao-tzu and Chuang-tzu's thinking with yin-yang philosophy, ritual, healing, and meditation at the end of the Han dynasty between 140 and 220 C.E. During the next four centuries Taoism developed monasteries, an extended canonical scripture, and magnificent festivals for community renewal. The coming of Buddhism to China profoundly influenced Taoism and all of Chinese society.

- Religious Taoism developed various systems for peaceful living, long life, and healing between the second and seventh

# A Brief Introduction to Taoist Meditation

centuries C.E. The most important of these is the *Gold Pavilion* classic.

- Taoism was made equal with Confucianism only during the Tang dynasty (619–906). The emperors made Taoist texts a part of the official civil service examination. Princesses of the royal family became ordained practicing Taoists.

- Taoism experienced a religious reformation during the Song dynasty (960–1281), some four centuries before Europe did. As a part of this reformation, laypeople began to meditate and took a greater role in Taoist arts and festivals. China's religious reformation was far more positive and sweeping than Europe's some 400 years later.

- Martial arts and other popular forms of Taoism evolved throughout the provinces of south and central China during the Yüan (Mongol) and Ming dynasties 1281–1368 and 1368–1644, respectively. Wood-block printing, which developed well before the first press in Europe, made Taoist meditation, healing, and martial arts manuals widely available.

- During the Ch'ing (Qing) dynasty (1644–1912) and the modern period, secret societies, business associations, and Tong special interest groups used Taoist arts, qi meditation, and healing methods for social unity and cohesion. Healing by the use of qi (ch'i breath), qigong meditation, kung fu martial arts, tai chi exercises, and many other popular arts from the Taoist tradition continue to develop in the modern world.

- Today Taoism is one of the five officially sanctioned religious movements in the People's Republic of China. It is controlled by a special section of the State Religious Affairs Bureau, with a Taoist Association watching over its development. With Buddhism, Islam, and Protestant and Catholic Christianity, it is considered to be important enough in modern Chinese socialist society to have its shrines and holy places rebuilt and young Taoists trained at state expense, a part of the new "socialism with a special Chinese flavor."

The special status given to Taoism is due to its immense popularity with ordinary people everywhere in China. The early morning streets and parks of Beijing and other large and small cities are filled with young and old devotees, practicing tai chi and other exercises (including disco and ballroom dancing) before going to work. Taoist shrines and temples, like Buddhist, Islamic, and Christian shrines, are filled with pilgrims and tourists. On special festival days visitors must take turns entering the Taoist shrines because so many are attempting to crowd in and watch the Taoist festivities.

Centers for studying Chinese medicine and various healing methods that are associated with Taoism are also to be found throughout China. Acupuncturists and massage experts who use qi (ch'i, breath-energy), traditional herbal remedies, and visualization methods to heal are given far more scientific status than in the West. Controlled experiments are used to measure the effects of these various techniques in healing illness. Homeopathic, natural healing techniques, are studied as a complement to Western medicine.

Following are some other sources for understanding more about Taoism from its prehistoric beginning until the present:

## Oracle bones and Ancient Writing

The written history of China begins with oracle bone inscriptions of the Shang-yin dynasty, 1760–1100 B.C.E. Inscribed on the back of tortoise shells and the leg bones of

# A Brief Introduction to Taoist Meditation

oxen, the oracle records show how the ancient kings of the Shang-yin dynasty invoked heaven before embarking on wars, journeys, burials, building projects, and recreational excursions such as hunting or visiting. The oracle writings ask about weather and success in warfare, hunting, or other royal projects by carving a question into the hard bone or tortoise shell and then applying heat to the surface of the bone or shell to call forth an answer.

Prayers to heal the ill in the king's immediate family occur frequently in the oracles. Illness is thought to be caused by the soul of an imperial ancestor or relative languishing in the underworld without prayer or sacrifice for relief. The notion that the merits, prayers, and good deeds of the living free the souls of the deceased from suffering, and thereby heal the illness of the living, remains a common Asian belief.

The oracle bones make a clear distinction between the spirits of the heavens who control weather, the spirits of the earth who govern nature, and the souls or demons in the afterlife-underworld who cause suffering and illness among humans. A triple world consisting of heaven, earth, and an underworld is deeply rooted in Chinese cosmology. Taoism addresses and "empties" the spirits of nature in later ritual.

## THE I CHING BOOK OF CHANGES

The Zhou (Chou) dynasty (1100–221 B.C.E.) left behind the earliest written records, first in the form of bronze and bamboo inscriptions, later in the written records of the Confucian tradition. The five classic books (the Books of Poetry, History, Spring-Autumn Annals, Rites, and the *I Ching*, the Book of Changes) are perhaps the oldest Chinese historical records. The

Confucian worldview permeates these works, a topic about which many fine studies in Western languages have been written.[12] The first two lines of each of the sixty-four chapters of the *I Ching* are among the oldest recorded Chinese documents.[13] The first lines of the *I Ching* are an important source for Taoist philosophy, meditation, and healing.

## Lao-tzu and Chuang-tzu (Laozi and Zhuangzi)

The Lao-tzu *Tao-te Ching* and the *Chuang-tzu* were most probably composed during the fourth century B.C.E.[14] The Lao-tzu book (summarized in chapter 2) is the first and foremost work given to the aspiring Taoist novice to read. Taoist meditation, ritual, and healing are based on its understanding.

The *Chuang-tzu* is the basic text of the Taoist meditative tradition. It is a very difficult text to understand or translate.[15] The book is divided into three parts: the Inner Chapters (1-7), probably composed by Chuang-tzu himself; the Outer Chapters (8-15), collated by his disciples; and the Miscellaneous Chapters (16–33), of later composition. The essence of the *Chuang-tzu* is contained in the humorous tales that accompany the rather obscure text. Some basic ideas from the *Chuang-tzu* are included in chapter 2.

## Taoist Schools

Religious Taoism, a mighty river fed by the mystic texts of Lao-tzu and Chuang-tzu, is joined by many other streams and rivulets from the second half of the Han dynasty, from about the beginning of the Common Era up until the Tang dynasty, which began in 619 C.E. Three greater sets of registers, lists of spirits' names used in ritual meditations, their

## A Brief Introduction to Taoist Meditation

appearance, talismans, and commands for summoning them and two lesser-known schools developed during this time:

*Dragon-Tiger Taoism*, also known as Zhengyi Celestial Master Taoism, is one of the earliest Taoist healing movements. Its founder, Zhang Daoling, the "first" celestial master, lived in the second century C.E. Dragon-Tiger or Zhengyi Taoists meditate on the Lao-tzu *Tao-te Ching* as a sacred book, practice rites of healing and renewal, and receive a special Zhengyi Mengwei (Cheng-i Meng-wei) register in twenty-four segments when they are ordained Taoists. Their sacred mountain is Lunghu Shan (Dragon-Tiger Mountain) in southeast Jiangxi Province. These Taoists marry and pass on their registers to at least one of their children in each generation.

*After meditation on the Thunder Spirits, Taoists draw talismans to heal, bring rain, heal illness. Zhengtong Taoist Canon woodblocks, ca. 1445.*

*Lingbao* (*Ling-pao*) and its registers are mentioned by a Taoist scholar named Ko Hong, in a work called *Baopuzi* (*Pao-p'u Tzu*, The Master Who Embraces Simplicity) in the early fourth century C.E. Lingbao Taoism teaches methods for healing and renewal based on the Five Talismanic Charms, the Lingbao Wufu. These talismans were used by the mythical emperor Yü, China's Noah, to stop the floods. Its sacred mountain is Gozao Shan, (Ge Tsao Shan) in southeast China.

*Highest Pure Shangqing Taoism* (*Shang-ch'ing*), reputedly founded by the woman mystic Lady Wei Huacun, teaches the healing and emptying meditations of the *Huang-t'ing Neijing* (the *Gold Pavilion* classic, Inner Chapters). Its sacred mountain is Mao Shan, twenty-five miles southeast of Nanjing in Jiangsu Province.

*North Pole Beiji Taoism* (*Pei-chi*) teaches meditations and martial arts for healing. It invokes Ursa Major, the constellation that points to the polestar, to exorcise harmful spirits and thoughts from the conscious and subconscious mind. Its sacred mountain is Wudang Shan (Wu-tang shan) in western Hubei Province near the Shaanxi border.

*Qingwei* (*Ch'ing-wei*), *Pure Refined Taoism* shares with the Tantric Buddhist orders of Tibet the use of thunder and lightning meditations for healing. Many of its mantras written in Siddham (that is, late Sanskrit chants) are similar to those used by Tendai and Shingon Tantric Buddhism in Japan, brought from China in the ninth century (Tang dynasty), and by Tibetan Tantric Buddhism.

Many of the healing methods used in these five kinds of classical Taoist "registers" became a part of the popular healing tradition during the religious reformation of the Song

# A Brief Introduction to Taoist Meditation

dynasty, 960 to 1281 C.E. Inspired perhaps by the spirit of simplicity found in the Lao-tzu and Chuang-tzu, the laity (ordinary people) derived ways of healing that simplified the complicated methods of the ordained Taoist priest. The *Gold Pavilion* classic contains some of these techniques and registers.

*Quanzhen* (ch'üan-chen) Taoism, a sixth great tradition, known as All True Taoism, was founded during the Song and popularized during the Yüan and subsequent eras, including the People's Republic today. Quanzhen Taoism's headquarters are at the Baiyun-Guan temple in Beijing. Its monasteries are found all over China. Quanzhen monks and nuns practice celibacy and abstinence (vegetarian diet) in a disciplined way of communal life. Married laypeople too may follow this reformed way of Taoist chant, Zen (Chan) Buddhist-like meditation, and Confucian family virtue.

In today's socialist China only two of these Taoist traditions are officially recognized by the state. The Zhengyi tradition of Dragon-Tiger Mountain in southern China and the Quanzhen school in Beijing (northern China) are classified as the two official Taoist sects. Young Taoists trained in Beijing and elsewhere are taught this simplified distinction and remain for the most part unaware of the rich Taoist tradition while attending the state schools. The Taoist masters who live in the mountains, however, and the "fireside" married Taoists of the towns and countryside villages, preserve and teach the old apophatic "emptying" traditions.

*Redhat Taoism*, the kataphatic, filling or "imaging" tradition, also flourished and continues to develop from the Song dynasty reformation until the present.[16] This tradition, however,

*The Gold Pavilion*

❊

does require an expert such as a possessed medium, shaman, Redhat saigong, or Bon priest, to do the exorcistic healing. It can be described but is not easily imitated, nor is it to be tried by the Western or Chinese reader.

The Taoist apophatic tradition, a practice that based healing and meditation on kenosis or emptying, became a movement available to the ordinary person of China's countryside and villages during the Song dynasty reformation, continuing to the present. The use of the *Tao-te Ching* and *Chuang-tzu* as meditation manuals, qi meditation, color visualization, massage, herbal remedies, healthy exercises, all became a part of a popular Taoist movement, available to anyone who would learn it. There was no esoteric or secret learning preserved for an elite few. All that one needed to do, in the words of Chuang-tzu, was to learn to "sit in forgetfulness" and "fast in the heart," that is, abstain from judgment in the mind and selfishness in the heart, to learn healing. Fasting in the judgmental mind and a selfless heart brought health to the body and to the society around the practicing Taoist. Members of the village community were taught this simple healing system. The visualization of healing colors and the prayer of emptying ("heart fasting" and "sitting in forgetfulness") taught in chapters 3 and 4 are used as means to assist the layperson as well as the Taoist to live a long life of peace, happiness, and good health. They are useful in promoting wholeness, mental and physical well-being, and long life for those who come to the Taoist for healing.

## THE GOLD PAVILION CLASSIC

The *Gold Pavilion* classic has as its focus the Gold Pavilion, the "void space" above the kidneys at the body's center of

## A Brief Introduction to Taoist Meditation

gravity. The text itself has two parts. One, called the "Outer Chapters," (*Huang-t'ing Wai-ch'ing*) teaches a way of emptying meditation. The other, called the "Inner Chapters," (*Huang-t'ing Nei-ch'ing*) adds a list of spirits' names to be sent forth from the Taoist's body as a prelude to contemplating the Tao. Only the meditations (Outer Chapters) of the *Gold Pavilion* classic are presented in chapter 4.

This translation is based on a commentary originating from the Taoist Shangqing (Shang-ch'ing) tradition, a text given to the beginner by a Taoist master. The cryptic meaning can be translated only by using a commentary, called a *mijue* (*mi-chüeh*) manual.[17] The text can be translated on a word-for-word basis in three distinct ways: For the purely physical meaning; as a description of the circulation of qi breath and color in the internal alchemy tradition; and as a meditation of apophasis (emptying) in the "heart fasting" and "sitting in forgetfulness" tradition of Chuang-tzu described in chapter 2. Following the Shangqing Highest Pure tradition attributed to Lady Wei Huacun, the translation presented here in all cases follows the apophatic or emptying tradition. It is from this last way that the Taoist method of peace, healing, and long life is mastered.

## Chapter Two

# Interior Peace

The writings of the ancient Taoist masters tell us that healing must begin from within the self. When the mind, heart, and body work as one harmonious unit in tune with nature, a new inner peace emerges. The mind is no longer ruffled by the criticism or praise of changeable human associates. This new self is not worried by blame, avoids praise, makes no negative or harmful judgments, in fact avoids making any judgment at all. The rules for this kind of life filled with Taoist harmony are found in the books of Lao-tzu and Chuang-tzu.

The book of Lao-tzu, the *Tao-te Ching* is a brief eighty-one paragraphs. When a novice approaches a Taoist master to become his or her disciple, the master insists on three things: read and practice the book of Lao-tzu; take the vows or promises of the Taoist way of life; and reject any fame, glory, or wealth accruing from the way of self-cultivation that the master teaches.

These three rules may at first seem excessive. Without

understanding the *Tao-te Ching*, one cannot follow the way of emptying meditation. Without practicing the Taoist way of life, self-healing is impossible. The simplicity and selflessness of the Taoist way of life preclude accepting any recompense for healing. The master warns the disciple that wisdom cannot be purchased, as can a work of art or an education. To demand a price for healing is to turn a profit on illness. To do this would make the healer ill and his or her wisdom no longer priceless. No matter how simple the rules may seem, the Taoist novice must prove that he or she observes them before learning from the master.

The very first phrases of the *Tao-te Ching* state that the transcendent, eternal Tao cannot be spoken about. "The Tao that is spoken is not the eternal Tao." If one calls it *wu*, nonbeing or transcendent being, then the role of Tao as gestating heaven and earth is named. If one calls it *yu*, holding on or pregnant, then Tao is seen as a mother giving birth to nature. Therefore, if one would know the ultimate, transcendent Tao from within, one must let go, *wu*, be entirely empty. If one looks outward contemplating the *yu*, infinite variety of things in the universe, one can see "mother" Tao nourishing the greatest and smallest things of nature.

Any judgment, that is, the joining of a noun or concept with a verb, is relative. To say "He is short" is a judgment. A person is only relatively tall or short, a work relatively hard or easy, the Tao *wu* (transcendent) or *yu* (immanent). "A speaker needs a listener," "Before has an after," "What goes up must come down," are examples of relative judgments. One should try instead not to make any judgment. Meditation is best that does not put a verb to a noun. When judgment is suspended, then one suddenly becomes finely tuned to the workings of Tao in nature. Beginning with this state of suspended judgment, one begins to learn Taoist healing meditation. This meditation is not done through the mind's knowing or by the heart's willing but in the belly's power of intuition and direct awareness of a transcendent presence.

I use the word *transcendent* here not in the connotation that many Western sinologists assign the word, but simply as a convenient way to avoid using the cliché "nonact" or "nonbeing," since, in the true Taoist use of the word, the Tao of *wuwei* "gives birth" to *taiji*, yang, yin, and the myriad creatures. This manner of act is called transcendent, rather than nonact, in these pages.

The Taoist way of contemplating is described in the texts of the Lao-tzu and Chuang-tzu summarized below. Its goal is to achieve a peaceful and tranquil mode of existence both when contemplating Tao's presence and when living an ordinary daily life.

## Lao-tzu on Healing

### Meditating on Nature

Nature does not "hold on" like humans do to possessions or judgments. Nature makes no judgments. It gives birth and lets go, does its work and moves on. When we sit in quiet contemplation and suspend judgment, we see Tao working in nature, the Taoist master teaches. We begin to understand how to contemplate, to look without making judgment. When we cease to make judgments, time passes quickly. An hour seems like less than a minute. The person who stops making negative judgments does not grow old mentally, and sees much more deeply into the world of the inner self and into the outer world of nature.

## Meditating on Emptiness

The person who becomes adept at not passing judgment soon becomes very peaceful. There is no need to flatter the powerful, pander to the wealthy, or lust after beauty in things or people. Inner peace of heart is more precious than all these external things. People with power, wealth, and beauty come to the Taoist to be healed of their inner cares and turmoil. The Taoist master teaches from chapter 3 of the *Tao-te Ching* that it is more important to:

> *Empty the heart-mind, fill the belly,*
> *Weaken selfishness, strengthen the bones,*
> *Let go, Tao will rule!*

The Tao that breathes life and beauty into nature is like a bowl filled with good things that are never used up. These good things of nature sprout in spring, ripen in summer, are harvested in fall, and "die" in winter, a cycle repeated annually in nature. Morning's dawn, noonday heat, evening's sunset, night's rest are a smaller version of human birth, growing up, maturity, old age, and death. Life is a process of giving and emptying.

Nature's Tao blunts the sharp edges in our lives, unties the knots, gives from its bowl of plenty. Tao is as equally at home with the bright and fresh as with the soiled and dusty. By suspending our judgments of what is good and bad in others, or

*Interior Peace*

how they approve and disapprove of our lives, we become suddenly aware that Tao does not have favorite people. We must be like Tao, treat all things in heaven and earth as sacred objects.

## Meditating on Tao as a Nourishing Mother

The Tao of nature is like a mother who is always spinning forth primordial energy, *yuanqi* (*ch'i*) or life breath, nurturing all things in nature.¹ She eternally gives this life breath, qi, to all of

*The "three fives" are joined together in the Yellow Court or Gold Pavilion and contemplate Tao. Ch'ing dynasty woodblock print from* Xingming Guizhi. *Left column text: jing, qi, shen depend on me to be joined as one. Right column text: body, heart, mind, who ever separated them?*

nature and never plays favorites. Tao always nourishes, eternally spins forth life breath, because it does not use up its qi in judgmental thoughts and selfish desires. This is why it can heal and does not die.

## Meditating on Qi

Healing life power for the Taoist is called qi, primordial life breath. Each of us has life breath within us, stored in the belly (the lower cinnabar field) and regenerated in the pineal gland (the upper cinnabar field) in the brain. During the day we use up our life energy each time we make a judgment, lust after something with desire, worry, are angry or sad. Life breath is restored each night by sleeping, and during the day by meditating and by qi exercise.[2] Qi exercise and meditation are important daily practices in the Taoist healing tradition.

## Meditating on Water

Water is a very important concept in the Taoist healing and meditation system. With qi energy it symbolizes the action of Tao in nature. Water always seeks the lowest place, can fit into any space, and brings life to all living things. Though it is soft and yielding, nothing can withstand its power, not even the strongest metal or hardest stone. Since water always seeks the lowest place, it is closest to Tao. Since it is supple and yielding, water does not "contend," fits any container, and always attains its goal. Thus we are told to meditate on and be like water in our daily lives.

*Interior Peace*

## Meditating on Heaven's Way

*Know when enough is too much.*
*A blade too sharp will soon be dulled,*
*A room full of gold will soon be emptied.*
*Let it go! Do your work and move on.*

It is the way of heaven and the four seasons to do their cyclical work and move on, never holding on to the good things of nature's abundance. Spring gives rain for plowing and planting. Summer gives heat for ripening. Autumn gives up its abundance in the harvest. Winter is for rest and contemplation. Nature always lets go of the good things it produces. Too much of any one thing brings floods, droughts, rotting crops, and freezing.

Moderation is a strict rule for the Taoist way of health. Never eat or drink too much. Always stop short before satiety in eating, and maintain sobriety in drink. The Taoist master will accept a modest drink of alcohol at a banquet or when toasting a guest, but ordinarily does not drink strong spirits. Monastic Taoists do not eat meat, fish, eggs, or milk products but do use garlic, spices, onions, and pepper. The rule of not eating meat is not absolute. When invited to a banquet or to a family feast, it is better not to offend the host. Taste small bits of meat or fish proffered at a banquet. Know how to stop before becoming full.

The rule of Buddhist ascetics forbids for religious reasons the use of spices and meat or other living creatures. For health's sake, the Taoists do not eat animal substances, but they do occasionally partake of meat when invited to a banquet, or when not to do so would offend the host. The rule of good manners, respecting the other, and positive judgment are always foremost in Taoist manners.

## Meditation on a Child

"Be like a child," the Taoist master teaches. A newborn child cries all day and is never hoarse. It has no hangups on sex. It eats, sleeps, does not carry weapons or contend. It does not get stung by bees or mauled by tigers. Its bones are soft, but its tiny fingers hold on to its mother with great strength. It is aware of breathing, does not say no, and thus can contemplate or "see" the transcendent Tao.

## Meditation on the Hollow Center

"Be like a mother's womb," give birth and nurture, and then let go. Be like the empty hub of a wheel. If the center of the wheel is not hollow, an axle cannot be inserted, and the thirty spokes of the wheel are useless; they cannot turn. A bowl must be hollowed out to hold water. A room must be uncluttered and have windows and doors to be lived in. Only when we are empty, unselfish, are we good to ourselves and others.

## Meditation on What's Inside

*Colors blind the eye, sound deafens the ear,*
*Flavors dull the taste, lust hurts the heart.*
*Value what is inside [Tao], not what is outside.*

When the mind is filled with colors, sounds, tastes, and sensations, it cannot be aware of the presence of the Tao deep down inside. Tao eternally gestates life breath in all of nature. When the mind is emptied of concepts and images and the heart lets go of desire for things, the work of the Tao gestating in nature can be observed by the instinctive powers of the belly. In Taoist philosophy the mind is for knowing, the heart for desiring, and the belly for intuiting or sensing. By meditating from the center of the belly rather than from the mind or heart, one can intuit Tao's presence.[3]

## Meditation on Life's Difficulties

One of the most important attitudes taught by Lao-tzu and Chuang-tzu is that disapproval, scoldings, opposition, and contradiction must be expected and welcomed as long as we are alive and functioning. "Be happy when scolded, fearful when praised," Lao-tzu jokingly warns us. By the very fact that we are alive and successful at our work, difficulties and contradictions come to us. If we were dead, then difficulties would not occur. So value opposition as you value your life. Run from praise and adulation with distrust. Do not depend for your self-image on what others think of you. Only when we are totally selfless, when we lose the need for praise or approval, can we be entrusted with ruling ourselves, our families, and the state. The *Chuang-tzu* (see later in this chapter) is filled with stories illustrating this principle.

## Meditation on an Uncarved Block of Wood

The uncarved block of wood is a symbol of simplicity used by Lao-tzu and Chuang-tzu. If the mind and heart are carved into pieces by arguments and worries, the body becomes ill. Chuang-tzu tells of a huge gnarled tree too twisted to be used for lumber. Because of this children come to play in its shadow and birds to nest and sing in its branches. Lao-tzu tells the Taoist healer to go wading in a cold winter creek, to shiver in its purifying coldness. Live in a crowded tenement without bothering the neighbors. Be thoughtful of the host's feelings when invited as a guest; be sensitive as thin ice about to melt in spring, unspoiled as the flowers in a wild meadow, clear like a pool of still water unruffled by wind, fresh like new green grass by the side of a stream. To do these things one must envision oneself as an uncarved block of wood.

### Meditation on a Good Ruler or Employer

Lao-tzu warns the Taoist healer that the best ruler, teacher, or healer is scarcely seen or known. The next best is loved, the third best is feared, and the worst is hated. If workers don't trust their employer or political leader, students their teacher, or patients their doctor, nothing lasting will be accomplished. The best ruler or healer says little, and when his or her work is done, the worker or patient says, "I did it." This is because healing must be in the patient, and work must be done by the worker.

### Meditation on Standing on Tiptoe

One cannot stand on tiptoe for very long, or walk very far on one's knees. Violent winds last less than a day and a torrential rainfall but a few hours. Heaven and earth make sure that violence does not last. Only when we are at peace within ourselves can we experience permanent health and wholeness. Food that is left over, deeds that require great and continual effort, a person who acts for glory and fame, are like people walking on tiptoe in a violent rain. None can last very long. Our hearts must be freed from all desires that are like a violent rainfall or walking on tiptoe, that bring tension and stress. Our minds must be purified of all violent and negative images in order to remain calm and constant. Good deeds should not be seen, and well-spoken words leave no target for envy. Lao-tzu jests:

> *Good accounting needs no ledger,*
> *Well-locked needs no key or bolt,*
> *Well-tied needs neither rope nor knot.*
> *The Taoist healer helps all,*
> *Turns none away, whether they are likeable or not.*

## Meditation on Healing

The Taoist healer turns no one away, weak, poor, crippled, or outcast, and never deliberately harms anything.[4] The person who is "one with the Tao" brings peace, great happiness, and nourishment for all, never rejecting anyone. When nourishing never try to preach or boss. "Be one with Tao" is the only message.

> *Because they are one with Tao,*
> *Heaven is bright, earth at peace,*
> *The soul is spiritual, the valley fertile,*
> *Nature gives birth, leaders pure and simple.*

## Meditation on Harmony

> *Tao gives birth to One [qi breath];*
> *One gives birth to Two [yang, heaven, male];*
> *Two give birth to Three [yin, earth, female];*

*These three gave birth to all other things.
It is because they are in harmony
That they can do this.*
   (*Tao-te Ching*, chapter 42)

## MEDITATION ON A HEALTHY BODY

The healer and the patient must realize that the body is the most important of our assets. The body's health is more important even than acquiring fame, wealth, and success in business. Profit and loss in business can bring on ailments. To fall madly in love is a great misfortune. The most successful person always leaves a little undone so that others too may succeed. The straightest line bends with the earth. One must move a little so as not to freeze, rest a little so as not to perspire. The person who does not bend becomes ill. Wait patiently for the best pottery, which comes last from the kiln. Listen quietly for the Tao from within the body's center, the belly, where the best music is silence. Those people are whole and endure who listen from within the body's center.

## MEDITATION ON GOODNESS

The person who would be a healer of other people's ills must be good to the kind and the unkind, true to the faithful and the unfaithful. Tao gives qi breath to all, plays no favorites, smiles on everyone. A person who is filled with goodness walks through the battlefield unscathed by death. The tiger's claws don't scratch, a sword doesn't cut, a bull doesn't maul goodness.

Goodness is defined by Lao-tzu as an interior quality that

## Interior Peace

helps all others, whether good or bad, loyal or unloyal, useful or useless. Like the Tao, it sees all things as sacred and looks on all as something in which Tao dwells.

### Meditation on Wuwei, Tao's Actions

The Tao makes little things important. To those with little it gives much. It requites anger with goodness, tackles difficulties at once, while they are still easy. It rewards three precious things: kindness, care, and those who do not put themselves over others. In fact, it rushes to the aid of those who show kindness. It helps each thing find its own way, never telling others what to do. Tao hides behind coarse clothes. It is to be found deep inside the meditator.

### Meditation on the Ocean

The reason the ocean is the greatest of all creatures is because it is the lowest. Therefore, everything flows into it. (*Tao-te Ching*, chapter 66)

### Meditation on Others

Never be weary of others, and they will not be weary of us. Our influence is greatest when others don't fear us and when we don't meddle in their lives at home. Meditate on all others with the greatest respect. When they come to see us, they will be better because of our respect.

### Meditation on Not Knowing

The most difficult things to heal are knowledge, concept, and image. Memories of what others have said about us, what injustices they have done, the images of what bad things could happen, fester in our minds and injure our stomachs. To heal, empty these concepts.

Disputes about philosophy and reason bring illness. The Taoist healer doesn't get ill, because he or she doesn't catch the "know-all" sickness. (*Tao-te Ching*, chapter 71)

MEDITATION ON BENDING

That which is dead is hard and brittle. That which is alive bends and is supple. To be healthy, be yielding like water, supple like grass, fresh and giving like Tao. Human ways are different from Tao. Humans in business and politics take from those who have little and give to those who have plenty. Tao gives of its plenty to all. Giving with joy makes one like Tao.

OF ALL THE eighty-one chapters of the *Tao-te Ching*, the religious Taoists consider chapter 42 (Meditation on Harmony, page 37) to be the most important. Qi, yang, and yin are able to give birth to the myriad creatures only because they work in harmony. In order that the people of the village who come to the temple for healing and renewal understand this message, the Taoists act it out in mime, drumming, music, and dance. The rite is as follows:

First, when it is dark, three new candles are set on an altar in the center of the temple for all of the villagers to see. If there are too many people to fit into the temple the table is brought out into the village square so that all can witness the drama.

Next, all of the lights in the temple are extinguished. The

*Interior Peace*

❂

Taoist strikes a new fire from flint and sings "The Tao gave birth to the One." At this point the first candle is lit. The Taoist chants how the first candle represents primordial breath, yuanqi, the breath of the Tao gestating. Then the second candle is lit for yang, and the third candle for yin. The reason the myriad creatures could be gestated, the Taoist chants, is because these three shine together in harmony.

At this point all of the lights, candles, and lanterns in the temple are lit, so that the night becomes as day. Tao gestating the cosmos is acted out in song and dance. The forty-second chapter, on harmony, is thus brought to the attention of the whole village by a rite that anyone—children, elders, and foreigners—can understand, even if they have never read the obscure text of the *Tao-te Ching*. Ritual is thus a vehicle to explain the philosophy of Lao-tzu.

## Meditations on the Chuang-tzu

The Lao-tzu *Tao-te Ching* is the first book given to an aspiring Taoist to follow. The *Chuang-tzu* is used at the next stage of meditative practice, as a prelude to the third and highest level of apophatic emptying meditation, found in the *Gold Pavilion* classic. Following the practice of the Taoist contemplative tradition, I have paraphrased here the first seven chapters of the *Chuang-tzu*, as a prelude to learning the meditations of apophasis.

The *Chuang-tzu* is one of the most literary and highly respected works of Chinese literature. Confucian, Buddhist, and Taoist scholars all attempt to read and comment on its difficult passages. The mystic philosophy it proposes for the reader is explained in humorous stories and parables, based on the teachings of Lao-tzu. The first seven chapters are considered the most important for the master of Taoist healing. Some of its major ideas and the stories that explain them follow.[5]

## Wandering in the World of Relative Judgment

> *Once there was a great fish that lived in the depths of the northern sea. Its name was Kun. Its back was more than a thousand li [Chinese miles] long. Suddenly it changed into a bird whose name was Peng, whose back was also more than a thousand li in length. Startled, the bird took off from the sea and flew away. Its wings obscured the whole sky like a cloud. This bird, flying over the skies, eventually journeyed to the southern realm, the lake of heaven.*

Ji Xie, a historian of the exotic, recorded the following: "When Peng took off for the south seas, its wings first flapped just above the water for three thousand li. Then it rose on an updraft to ninety thousand li. Its flight lasted for six months; then it rested."[6]

All judgments are relative to the judger. We must not use the great Peng bird as a standard to judge small birds. Water deep enough to float a cup is not sufficient to hold a boat. Peng's wings touched the water as it flapped, until it reached a height of ninety thousand li. The cicada and the dove do not need so much space to fly. Kun the great fish (a symbol of yin, autumn and winter) changed to Peng the great bird (yang, spring and summer). Each has its function in nature. One is not

*Interior Peace*

❁

better than the other. We think they are different, but in fact one changes into the other.

All human judgments are relative to the judger. A mushroom sprouts in the morning and does not last a month, while a butterfly lives for a season. A magic mushroom in the southern Chu state lives a thousand years, and the *dachun* tree for two thousand. A tree or a person is not good or bad because of how long it lives or how people judge and talk about it.

Some people have enough talent to do well in a small business, while others rule a company. Others yet become governors of an entire kingdom. The whole world may admire one of these and despise the other two. Yet they are no better or worse within themselves for what others say about them or judge them to be. Liezi (Lieh-tzu) was a great Taoist sage who could ride off on the wind for fifteen days at a time. Yet Liezi depended on the wind to move, just as ordinary men depend on their legs to walk. What if there were someone who could mount into the heavens and descend into the earth, ride the six breaths of change (cold, heat, drought, rain, wind, fire), and wander in the transcendent ultimate (Tao)? Would this person make Liezi look bad? In fact, the person who has truly attained the Tao is selfless. The true spiritual person has no merit. The holiest sage has no fame. What others say of them is irrelevant.

There was once a spiritual person who lived in the Guyi Mountains. Though very old, his skin was like snow and his body young and graceful. He did not eat any of the five starches but subsisted on wind and dew. He could ride away on clouds of qi breath, his chariot a flying dragon, into the world beyond the four seas, outside the realm of Confucian logic. The most important thing about this person, Chuang-tzu states, was his inner peace of spirit. His presence harmonized village life and nature. The villagers who lived nearby were saved from illness and each year harvested good crops.

This last quality alone was for Chuang-tzu the sign of the true Taoist sage. No matter what powers and virtues are extolled in the sagely person, it is because of interior peace alone that his or her presence brings blessing. Inner peace heals all natural and human calamities.

King Yao, after visiting the holy sage of Mount Guyi, decided to give up his kingdom.[7] All the good things that come to the ruler of a kingdom were useless when compared with the inner peace of meditation. He compared the goods of the kingdom to a merchant who tried to sell fancy hats and shirts to the people of the southern kingdom of Yueh. The people of Yueh had no use for hats or shirts. They tattooed their bodies with bright colors instead. The values of Confucians, politicians, and modern consumer society are wasted on those who live lives of peaceful simplicity.

Huizi asked Chuang-tzu what to do about a huge gnarled tree that could not be sold to carpenters for wood. Plant it in the realm of wuwei (Taoist action), Chuang-tzu replied, and go there to meditate. A thing that is useless will not be harmed by the world of politicians, consumers, or war. The values of consumer society chop down all things (and all people too) who seem useful for making a profit. The preservation of nature, a peaceful society, and a healthy human body are more important than profit.

## Interior Peace

### On Abstaining from Judgment

A famous Taoist sage named Nan Guozi Ji (Nan kuo-tzu Chi) was meditating peacefully while sitting at a table. He looked up to heaven while practicing quiet breathing. In doing this, he seemed to have suspended his conscious judgmental mind.

His friend Yan Chengzi Yu stood in front of him and asked, "Are you still there? Can the body's form become dry wood and the mind like dead ashes? This person meditating by the table is not the same person who was here meditating a while ago."

"Yan," said Nan Guozi Ji, "It's a good thing that you ask me about it. Just now I had forgotten to make judgments. Would you like to know how its done? You've heard the sound of human music played on the flute, but not the sound of the earth's flute. If you hear the music of the earth's flute, you still haven't heard the music of heaven's flute!"

Yan asked Nan to continue. The sound of the earth's flute, Nan Guozi Ji explained, is heard in the wind playing on the hollows of trees, caves, mountains, and valleys. The sounds of earth are sometimes soft and quiet, sometimes loud and strident. The sounds of heaven's flute are heard only when all other sounds cease. One must listen to the intervals between the sounds of earth and humans to hear the music of heaven.

The sounds of human music are made on flutes and vocal chords. Human words produce arguing, judging, agreeing, and disagreeing. Human sounds are more strident than the violent storms of earth. When humans compete with each other, there are plotting and scheming, indecision and concealment, apprehension and distress, reserve and fear. The human mind is like a spear that flies forth deciding what is right and wrong. Some minds are firm, others change like weather. Some are mired in sensuous pleasure, others are plugged with hardened ideas like an old drain, unable to be cleared.

Nan Guozi Ji compared human joy and anger, sorrow and pleasure, anxiety and regret, whimsy and resolve, violence and laziness, indulgence and extravagance, to the sounds of nature's flute, short-lived as mushrooms sprouting after a rain. Day and night our feelings sprout from within us. They keep us from hearing Tao's music.

A monkey keeper in a Zoo once ordered that the monkeys be given three bananas each morning and four bananas each evening. This made the monkeys very angry, since they thought the three bananas were not enough. So the keeper ordered that four bananas be given in the morning and three at night. The monkeys were happy at this decision.

Judging whether one idea is better than another, or (as philosophers did in Chuang-tzu's time) whether a pure white horse is a different breed than all other kinds of horses, is like monkeys arguing over bananas. It is like saying that eyes are more important than ears, or the upper part of the body better than the lower. Without the viscera we could not live. Nothing in the world of itself is better than any other thing. Judging and feeling a thing to be good or bad obscures the music of Tao in the cosmos. Tao is obscured by distinction, partiality, and eloquence. Tao is known when there is no distinction, partiality, or judgment. It is the truly wise person who sees that human feelings and judgments are simply a declaration of preference and wishes, like a monkey upset about three bananas in the morning and four in the evening. It is the deepest of insights that sees how the elements of one's physical body came into being with the cosmos. Life and death are simply different ways of relating to the cosmos. In this sense, Chuang-tzu asks us to consider how:

> *Heaven, earth, and I were born together.*
> *The myriad creatures and I are one.*
> *All have this, our existence, in common.*

Tao makes no distinctions in gestating the myriad creatures. Only humans make distinctions about the value of things in their speech and judgments. In all, there are only eight possible choices: be on the right or the left, discuss or judge, divide or argue, emulate or contend. The sage does not choose sides, argue, judge, or contend.

Is there anything, Wangyi was asked, on which everyone can agree? [8] Humans live in houses, he answered, monkeys in trees, eels in damp places. Deer eat grass, centipedes eat snakes, owls and crows eat mice. Mao Jiang and Li Ji were reputed to be two beautiful women, but when fish and birds saw them they fled. The Taoist sage does not judge one person better or worse for their preferences, or declare herself or himself more wise, benevolent, or chaste than others. The sage never harms anyone, does not pursue worldly affairs, does not dispute or argue about distinctions, and ignores all differences in social rank.

Those who follow worldly ways see an egg and immediately expect to see it hatch and hear the bird crow. They see a crossbow and immediately want to sit down to a banquet after the hunt. Princess Li Ji cried when she was sent to marry in the distant state of Jin. But when she got there and shared the luxurious court life with the king, she repented her tears. People who fear death are like those who run away when young and fear to return home. The sage's home is in the cosmos. Eternity has already begun.

"Suppose" Chuang-tzu says, "That I argue with you and you with me. . . . If one of us loses and one of us wins, which one of us is right and which one wrong?" Agreeing with someone does not necessarily make that person right. Disagreeing does not make the other person wrong. It is best to forget arguing. Let others be themselves, without forcing them to conform to one's own idea or dream of how things should be.

Our dreams are filled with illusions. Sometimes we dream of a banquet and wake up to an empty stomach. At other times we dream of monsters, failure, and violence. Chuang-tzu changes the bad thoughts to peaceful and quiet images. Life itself is a great dream, the images of which we can change at will.

> *Once Chuang-tzu dreamed he was a butterfly, fluttering about enjoying itself. It did not know it was Chuang-tzu. Suddenly it woke up, and was Chuang-tzu again. We are not sure if it was Chuang-tzu dreaming he was a butterfly, or the butterfly dreaming he was Chuang-tzu. This is called* hua, *changing dreams.*

We are what we make our dreams to be. If we dream a bad dream, it is important to change the bad images to good ones. When we dwell on calamities or successes, we become what we envision. Healing means making the image good, removing anger, fear, and bitterness. To hear the flute of

*Interior Peace*

heaven, as Nan Guozi Ji did at the beginning of this meditation, we must empty the mind not only of negative ideas but of all images and judgments. We thus "change" (*hua*) our dreams and visions so that our spirit becomes peaceful (*ning*), like the sage of Guyi Mountain. "Let us take our joy in the realm of the transcendent rather than in the argument;" listen to the flute of heaven rather than the flute of humans.

### The Master of Healthy Living

Once there was a butcher who was so good at carving that for nineteen years and two thousand bullocks he never once had to sharpen his knife. When asked by the king how his art had become so perfect, he answered:

> "What your servant loves most is Tao. There is no art greater than Tao. When I first became a butcher, what I saw in front of me was a piece of beef. After three years I saw the whole. Now I work with my *shen* [inner spiritual energy], not my eyes. The desire to know ended and the power of intuition was freed, by relying on heaven's way. . . . The joints of meat have empty spaces between the sinews, and the edge of the blade has no thickness. When that with no thickness is put into the empty space, . . . the meat comes apart by itself. . . ."
>
> "Excellent!" said the king. "From the words of this butcher I have learned how to nourish life!"

The person who loves Tao has learned how to contemplate, to use the power of intuition separately from the cognitive senses. The power of cognition or reasoning is mediated.

The external image is processed through the five senses into the imagination, from whence the bonds of concept, word, and judgment are formed. The Tao of the butcher moved freely through the void, empty spaces, unimpeded by the bones and sinews of the bullock. The king understood from this that the mind must be freed from the fetters of words and judgment to sense the movement or the "music" of the Tao in nature.

Knowing the Tao intuitively is the way to "nourish life." This nourishing is done by freeing the *shen* spirit, the power of will residing in the heart, from the bonds of the judgmental mind, from putting a verb to a noun, choosing between good and bad, making distinctions and preferences. This freedom of spirit and love of Tao can belong to anyone, even a person who is missing an arm or a leg.

A man who did not understand the Tao of heaven was startled to see that the king's favorite "minister of the right" was missing a foot.

"This is due to nature, not to man," replied the minister of the right. The Tao of heaven gives wisdom, peace, and good health to those whose spirit is free, not bound by the preferences and judgments of human society. "The wild pheasant in the marshes prefers to have one bite of grain every ten paces, and a sip of water every hundred steps, rather than be locked in a cage."

Health is maintained by having this free spirit, not bound by the values or conventions of what the world takes to be a perfect physical body. Freedom of spirit means freedom from all imposed styles, including clothing, body style, size, weight, shape, color, even physical disability and deformity. In a later

# Interior Peace

chapter Chuang-tzu finds Tao's special presence and blessing in the physically deformed, like the minister with one foot.

Fear of death, and excessive mourning are also forms of illness and bondage. When Lao-tzu died, his disciple Jinsi went to mourn. He uttered three loud cries and came away, embarrassed by the distant relatives who made endless loud lamentations. If they understood Lao-tzu's teaching, he said, they would not be mourning. Death is *di* (that is, God), letting go of the cord that binds us to time. There is no sense in mourning this release.

The master who nourishes life teaches freedom from bondage. Thoughts and judgments that bind us in fear are worse ills than missing a hand or a foot. The life fire inside us does not go out at death. When kindling wood is burned, fire moves on to burn somewhere else.

## Living in the Human World

When living in the human world, we cannot help but get caught up in the values, judgments, and worries of business and politics. Confucius sought to heal the evils of politics and commerce by teaching others, especially rulers and leaders, how to be virtuous. Lao-tzu and Chuang-tzu felt that such an approach brought only opprobrium and scorn, sometimes even death to the teacher.

Yan Hui asked Confucius's leave to go heal the ills of the state of Wei. The king of Wei refused to see his own or the country's problems. The dead lay in the street like the leaves of a dying banana tree. The sick crowded around the doors of physicians. Confucius warned Yan Hui that he would only bring suffering and misfortune on himself. The "perfect" person must first reach inner peace and not think of winning fame by changing wicked people. The power of virtue is spoiled by seeking fame.

"Desire for knowledge starts with contention. When competing for fame men crush each other, and knowledge is the weapon of their contention." Those who practice human virtues but don't understand the difference in nature and human ways try to force benevolence, justice, and law on the wicked. As a result, they are hated by the wicked and end up hurting others. Rulers kill virtuous ministers who try to help the welfare of the poor by changing the king's or lingdao's (the party boss's) evil ways.

Yan Hui suggested ways of changing his own behavior in order to be successful. All of these methods were rejected by Confucius. "Fasting in the heart-mind [*xinzhai*] is the only way," said Confucius.[9] He defines *xinzhai* as follows:

> *If zhi [the will] is kept one with Tao's presence within, then one no longer listens with the ears but with the heart. If one stops listening with the heart, then one can hear with qi life breath, and listening with the ears ceases. Listening with the heart ceases when it is unified [with Tao].*[10]
> The heart stops [listening to the ears] when it is united to Tao. The qi life energy is itself empty of image, waiting for things [to be brought into the mind through hearing and seeing]. Only the Tao dwells in the void! Fasting in the heart means that the heart-mind is emptied so that only the Tao may dwell there. Heart fasting is the only way to keep ourselves healthy in the world of humans. When the door is kept closed, poisonous things cannot enter.

## Interior Peace

✺

> *Keep the ears and eyes focused on Tao within, so that the mind is not filled with the human struggles for fame. Shut out wordly knowledge and judgments, lest spirits and demons come and dwell inside, along with the human world and its tensions.*

Only in this way, says Confucius, can Yan Hui survive in the evil state of Wei.

The Confucian way of benevolent virtue and the Taoist way of "fasting in the heart" are quite incompatible according to most ancient and modern scholars. Nevertheless, Chuang-tzu continues to use his created image of Confucius as the teacher for a healthy life in the world of humans. According to Confucius there are two great commandments. The first is for a child to love his or her parents, and the second is to fulfill one's duty to country and sovereign. These very human values certainly touch universal heartstrings. The Taoist way does not negate or dispute them. Rather, it adds a third principle. We must at all cost preserve our heart fasting, so that neither sorrow nor joy can affect inner peace, no matter what hardships or successes destiny brings into our life. This last rule is the perfection of all virtue.

In politics, sports, and drinking, things always begin with a show of friendship and end in mistrust, anger, and confusion. Politicians always sign treaties with a show of cooperation, but when they return home they begin to mistrust each other. Wrestlers begin their match by shaking hands but end in mutual rage, making sounds like animals in the throes of death. Banquets begin with toasts all around but turn into loud singing and brawling. A friendly argument can provoke brute ideas when one party is driven into a corner. There are many things in the world of humans that we cannot change for the better. Inner peace lets things develop each according to its own destiny, without letting the inner self be hurt by what cannot be changed, no matter how hard we may want to change or heal others.

Just as it is very important not to let external affairs penetrate into one's inner state of peace, so also it is very important not to let others see and envy one's inner harmony. Manifesting one's inner peace could make one into a hero or, worst of all, a holy "guru." This will lead to collapse, ruin, and personal downfall. Fame and reputation make one first into a sage, then into an oddball, and finally into an omen of evil.

In order to lead people to find healing peace within themselves, one should first become aware of their inner needs and feelings, and then lead them to their own discovery of heart fasting. When the sick person wants to act as a child, then we too must be like a child. When the patient wants to cast aside all differences, distinction, and judgments, then we too should cast them aside. The patient becomes the teacher, the sick person is the healer.

To show this point, Chuang-tzu tells three stories. The first is the tale of the praying mantis and the chariot. The praying mantis was very brave. It feared no adversary, and stood up to any attacker. One day a chariot came along and the mantis was crushed beneath its wheels. Rulers, *lingdao* (party bosses), and law enforcers are like the chariot that crushed the mantis. No matter how right we know ourselves to be, it is best to get out of the way of the powerful and the mighty. We may know that our inner peace and healing qi are excellent. But if we show

## Interior Peace

these good things to rulers and offend them, at best our own lives may be in danger. At worst, we may be drawn from our way of peace and stuck on the revolving chariot wheels of the powerful and mighty.

Tiger keepers in zoos and circuses understand the nature of their charges. They never feed live meat to the tigers, for fear of exciting their wild instincts to kill. When the tigers are no longer hungry, but are quite full, then they respect and obey their trainers. If one were to act against the rapacious or hunting nature of the tiger (or the ruler), one would be killed and eaten.

The same is true of those who train horses. The horse is a beautiful animal. It must be fed, combed, curried, and exercised every day. The trainer knows it is necessary to keep away from the hooves of the horses, lest he or she be kicked or injured when the horse is bitten by a fly.

The only way to heal human ills, too, is to keep oneself and the sick person away from what harms nature. One of the best ways of doing this is to learn how to be useless, that is, not injured, hurt, or destroyed by being "used" in the world of humans. This notion of being useless is, of course, a special term in the Taoist system. It does not mean being useless to our family, loved ones, or nature. To illustrate its meaning, Chuang-tzu tells a series of stories about trees, animals, and deformed humans.

Once there was a great oak tree that was used as a sacred altar for crop offerings in the state of Ji (Chi). This tree was so large that an oxcart when passing behind it could not be seen. It was one hundred yards in circumference, and were it not so gnarled and twisted, boats might have been hollowed out from at least eight of its branches. A master craftsman with his apprentices passed by one day. The apprentices wanted to chop the tree down and cut it up into lumber to make houses, ships, coffins, and furniture. The master carpenter would not listen to them, and passed by the tree quickly.

That night the tree appeared to the carpenter in a dream. The reason it had lived so long and not been cut down was because its wood was useless, the tree told the carpenter. All the other trees around had been chopped down for their lumber. The hawthorn, pear, orange, pomelo, and other fruit trees had been mercilessly beaten, their fruit broken off, and finally chopped down for firewood. But the old oak survived because it learned to be useless. "If I were useful, how could I have survived to become so great?"

The tree asked the carpenter if he too understood the meaning of being useless. A useless carpenter who would not outlive the tree knew better than to cut the useless tree.

When he awoke the carpenter told his dream to his apprentices. "How can it call itself useless when it serves as an altar for the soil spirit?" they asked. "The tree just pretends to be an altar," he answered, "for the sake of those who don't know that it is useless."[11]

The great trees that appear throughout the pages of the *Chuang-tzu* all have one thing in common. They cannot be used for lumber, houses, boats, coffins, firewood, or fruit production. Thus they are "useless" in the eyes of the merchant, carpenter, and householder. But they can be used for their shade, for children to play under, birds to nest in, and villagers to dance under. The spiritual person survives with this kind of uselessness. In ancient China oxen with white foreheads, pigs

*Interior Peace*

---

whose snouts turned up too sharply, and humans suffering from hemorrhoids could not be used as a living sacrifice to the Yellow River.[12] Thus, being deformed or standing out from the ordinary, being "useless," saves one's life from religious sacrifice, physical and social burnout.

Chuang-tzu tells of a useless deformed man named Shu whose body was so twisted that the government gave him three bushels of grain and ten bundles of firewood weekly and never called him for wartime draft or peacetime corvée labor. Confucius is warned by the madman of Chu that his attempts to reform human society by his virtue are dangerous. One must avoid being useful, or one will be cut down for firewood, fried in the pan like good oil, eaten like fruit or cinnamon bark, worn out by the burdens imposed on oneself by claims to usefulness and notoriety. To be "useless" (*wu yong*) is a spiritual quality. "No use" in fact becomes "transcendent use," used by the Tao of nature to heal others. Thus "no use" means "Tao use," a person at one with nature.

## Virtue that Fulfills Tao's Fu Contract

Chuang-tzu tells many stories of people who lost their feet or toes or were deformed and ugly. All found interior peace by realizing that death and life, peril in living, good and bad fortune, wealth and poverty, being valued or thought worthless, praise and blame, are part of the destiny of being human. "One should not let such things disturb one's peace. One should not allow such things to enter the mind." Remain peaceful, kind, and content with the outer world as it is. Changes in the exterior world cannot affect Tao's interior stillness and peace. Such a person is "one with Tao's peace by contract."

In the state of Lu (Confucius's home) there was a man named Wang Dai who had only one foot. His disciples were more numerous than those of Confucius. He did not use words to teach or discuss. His disciples came to him empty and went away filled with good. The followers of Confucius asked how this could be. Even though his body was deformed, could his heart and mind be perfected? How could he teach without words?

Confucius answered that he, indeed, and all of his disciples should go to learn from the man with one foot. "Death and life are great events, but they cannot change him. If heaven fell and earth were disrupted, he would not be affected. His mind is like jade with no veins or flaws [not flawed by negation or attachment], and thus he does not let his interior [peace] be moved when exterior things change.[13] It is the destiny of things to change; thus he keeps his focus on the [unchanging] ancestral Tao."

The symbol of union between the heart of the meditator and the eternal Tao is compared here to a contract that unites two halves of a talisman. The *tao* (*dao*) or heavenly half, and the *te* (*de*) or interior half of the meditator are always united into one. The changes of the exterior world do not affect this union.

"If we see things from the viewpoint of distinction and difference," continued Confucius, "then the liver and the gallbladder are as far apart as the kingdoms of Chu and Yueh [the provinces of Hubei and Fujian in north central and southeast China, respectively]. If we see all things as united [by Tao's gestating and nourishing], then the myriad creatures are one."

## Interior Peace

The man with one foot kept his heart united with the presence of Tao. He did not let his ears and eyes become attached to the sounds and colors of the changing world. When all things are seen as one process, the loss of a foot or the loss of life itself is like the recycling or returning of so much earth. Only the truly virtuous (*de* or true virtue here means union with Tao's process) have minds that are clear like still water. Minds running in the world of humans are like a turbulent muddy stream. They cannot find peace, even if the body has two feet and appears to be whole.

To be in the world of humans is like standing in the middle of a battlefield where arrows are flying. One cannot help one's destiny or be perturbed by being hit. If one wanders in the center of the battlefield, one is more likely to be injured than if one wanders in the interior world of peace. But whether one is injured, loses a foot, becomes ill, or remains whole, the inner awareness of union with Tao's gestation of the cosmos need not be affected. The difference lies in whether the meditator is distracted by the goods of the outer world or is absorbed in the presence of Tao within.

Once there was a man named Aidaido. He was ugly enough to scare the whole world. Yet he was so peaceful inside that everyone trusted him. Men who were his friends felt comfortable only in his presence. Young women said to their parents, "I'd rather be his concubine than another man's wife." The king asked him to be prime minister, but he turned the job down and went away.

This kind of person considers knowledge and power a curse, conventionality as glue, moral virtue as a ruse to get one's way, and art as a form of commerce. Such a person does not rule and so needs no power, does not divide things and so needs no glue. His or her character is kind and never harms others, and thus needs not follow the conventions of socially approved "benevolence" and "reciprocal obligation." Such persons are nourished by nature and so need no consumer goods or commercial art. They do not have "affection" or attachments and so do not use others to succeed or get their way. Such persons are small and insignificant in human society but great and unique in their oneness with nature.

"How can a person be without attachment?" Huizi asked Chuang-tzu.

Chuang-tzu answered that people without attachment do not inflict internal injury on themselves by losing awareness of Tao within, or external injury on others by desires and aversions. "Tao gives us our face. Nature gives us our external appearance. We harm our inner self by saying 'I like it' or 'I hate it'." Tao gives us our being to rejoice in. Nature gives us our form to accept. If one wastes one's energies trying to change others' behavior in the external world, one's qi vital energy is soon used up. Change one's inner self instead by becoming peacefully aware of Tao's presence. Virtue means to see what is beneficial and what is harmful in the external world as one. Neither should destroy our sense of inner peace and harmony.

## Tao Is the Great Ancestral Master

The sixth chapter of the *Chuang-tzu* defines the nature of a Tao-realized person, the *zhenren*. Literally the Chinese phrase means "true person," one who is always aware of the presence of Tao in nature. To know the Tao means to empty the mind of all other images. Nothing else can be in the mind or heart when

## Interior Peace

Tao is there. The zhenren is a person who has realized this unity of heart with Tao.

A true person (Tao-realized person) is one who does not side with the majority or oppose the minority, who has made no plans or schemes to harm or put down others, who does not regret failure and is not self-complacent in success. He or she can climb mountains without fear of heights, walk in water without fear of getting wet, be near fire or desert heat without feeling hot. Such is the person whose heart and mind are one with Tao.

Tao-realized zhenren of the past, Chuang-tzu says, were people who

> did not dream when sleeping and did not worry when awake. They did not eat fancy things, and took long deep breaths. Zhenren inhaled through their heels, while ordinary people breathed through the throat. The selfish desires of ordinary people went so deep that their connections with heaven and Tao were shallow.
>
> Long ago the Tao-realized did not know attachment to life or fear of death. Birthing was not theirs to assent to, and dying not theirs to refuse. Yet they did not forget their beginning [from Tao] nor seek to know what their end would be. They received joyfully what was given and made good what was forgotten. They did not let the mind harm Tao's inner presence and did not use humans to try to change heaven. This is the definition of a zhenren, a person who has realized Tao.

Tao-realized people forget, that is, free themselves from thoughts of fame in the world of people. In warfare they would rather lose the kingdom than hurt people (that is, the presence of Tao in their hearts). Their good deeds benefit a myriad generations without looking to favor any one specially "loved" person. They are benevolent to all, not just loved ones. Their wisdom is constant, unlike changing weather. For them personal profit and loss are equally unimportant.

Life and death are part of a single journey home, in which we help each other walk along the way. When a stream dries up, the fish all come together in little puddles, keeping each other moist with their bodies. But their lives are better when they can forget each other's ills and swim off healthily in a great lake. Our minds filled with worries are like fish in a dried-up stream, without water to swim in. Once minds are emptied, the waters of the universe flood in again. We can swim away in good health, forgetting our own and others' ills, dissolved in the great ocean, the Tao-gestated cosmos.

Worldly knowledge, as in Lao-tzu's meditation in the *Tao-te Ching* is an illness that dries up the ocean of life around us.[14] It can be compared to a boat or a fisherman's net hidden in a river at night, supposedly safe from a thief's hand. But our knowledge, good health, and wealth can be taken from us, just as the boat or net can be stolen. There is nothing in the universe, big or small, that cannot be destroyed or taken away. Only if we store things in the universe itself can they never be lost. The universe carries us through our bodies, toils in us through our life, slows us down in old age, and gives us repose in death. Nothing in the greater universe can be lost, and everything in the universe is good. It makes life good, and death good too. The "realized person" makes excursions into Tao, which cannot be lost, and takes joy in remaining together with it.

Chuang-tzu defines what Tao is:

> Tao has feeling and trust; it is transcendent act and transcendent form. It can be passed on but not received, it can be interiorized but not seen. It is its own origin and its own roots. It existed before heaven and earth, spirit-demons, or spirit-gods. It gave birth to heaven and earth. It is prior to taiji [t'ai-chi, the Great Ultimate],[15] but not too high, and the six directions, but not too deep.[16]
> Born prior to heaven and earth but not timeworn, older than ancient antiquity but not aged.

Chuang-tzu gives a long list of ancient sages who attained the Tao and were thereby able to fulfill the course nature appointed for them. The sun and moon have Tao and are therefore constant in their course. The Big Dipper constellation has it, and so always points to the center of the northern heavens. Just as the Big Dipper always points to the center of the northern heavens, so we too should always be aware of Tao in the center of our body. The oneness of body and the polestar is one of the most important of Taoist meditations.[17]

Zikuei asked Nu Ju, "How can your countenance be like a child, when you are so old?"

"I am acquainted with Tao," Nu Ju said. Because he had Tao, Nu Ju could

> Disregard all worldly affairs,
> Forget all external things,

> *Overlook his own existence,*
> *And be enlightened by the vision*
> *Of the "One" Tao.*
> *He no longer distinguished*
> *Past and present,*
> *Life and death . . .*
> *And was able to be peaceful*
> *No matter what disturbance. . . .*
> *He learned all this from enjoying*
> *The mystery of the eternal Tao.*

Once there were four friends named Zisi, Ziyu, Zili, and Zilai (self-aware, self-possessed, self-respect, and self-arrived). All four were friends, because all realized that death and life, existence and nonexistence, were all one process. One by one the friends fell ill and began to die. Each passed away without sorrow or joy, realizing that death was a release from bondage. The last of the friends, Zilai, said, "If we take the universe as a great furnace, and nature as a great alchemist, what place is it not right for us to go? Calmly we die, as quietly we live." These and the other Taoist sages were "companions of the maker of things." Their death was "an excursion into the unity of the universe." For them death was but a change of lodging.

Yan Hui explained to Confucius the meditation of "sitting in forgetfulness" (*zuowang*).

> *My limbs do not feel,*
> *My mind is darkened,*
> *I have forgotten my body*
> *And discarded my knowledge.*

## Interior Peace

❊

*By so doing,*
*I have become one*
*With the infinite Tao.*

Ziyu and Zisang were friends. Once it rained for ten days. Ziyu was afraid that his friend Zisang might be without sustenance, so he packed some food and went to take care of him. As he approached his friend's door, he heard Zisang complaining. "My father, mother, nature, and all men have abandoned me," he sang, while playing on a small lute. "Heaven covers and earth supports all things equally. What fate of mine is it to be so abandoned!" Little did he realize that his friend was at the door with healing food and care. Sitting in forgetfulness of self makes the healer able to see from afar and come to look after the needs of others.

### King Tai's Response to Tao

Once Yuejue asked Wangyi four questions:

*Do you know in what all things agree?*
*Do you know what you don't know?*
*Do all things have no knowledge?*
*If you don't know what is good and what harmful, is*
*the perfect person without this knowledge?*

To all four questions Wangyi answered that he didn't know. Instead he said that the perfect person did not fear extreme heat or cold, lightning or storms, death nor life. How could he worry about what was good or harmful?

Yuejue was delighted with this answer and went to tell Puyizi about it. Puyizi told of the ancient King Tai's response to such questions:

*Asleep he was tranquil, awake at peace.*
*He took himself to be the same as a horse or a cow.*
*He knew human feelings and trust.*
*His virtue was so deep that he didn't distinguish "good" and "bad" in humans.*

Trying to make rules so everyone will practice virtue is like trying to wade in the depths of the ocean, chop a path through a river, or make a mosquito carry a mountain. The sage lets all persons do what they do best, without forcing everyone to be the same.

Once Heaven Root was strolling on the sunny side of Mount Yin, just above the river Liao. He met Nameless and asked him how to govern the world.

"Go away, worthless thing," replied Nameless, "I'm too busy riding on the Great Bird [the Peng bird described earlier], beyond the six directions, wandering in a nonplace, in the domain of nothingness. How dare you disturb me with the worries that fill the heart with controlling the world?"

Realizing that he had come to the right place and the right person, Heaven Root asked the question again. Nameless answered:

*Wander with the heart-mind empty,*
*Join your qi breath with nothingness [nonjudgment],*
*Let all things follow their own nature,*
*And have no selfish interests.*
*Then the whole world will rule itself.*

Chuang-tzu relates how Lao-tzu once said that the wise ruler should not be like a servant or artisan, toiling with all

*Interior Peace*

one's strength and wearing out the heart and mind. Tigers and leopards are hunted for their skins. Monkeys and dogs are tied up because they are useful and clever. None of these make wise rulers. The ruler who responds to Tao has the greatest achievement in the world but does not claim it to be his or her own glory or possession. The ruler heals all who come for help, but no one thereby becomes dependent on him or her thereafter. Rather they learn self-healing and joy from within themselves. Like their healer they stand in the presence of Tao's mystery and make excursions into the infinite.

Once there was a noted spirit medium named Zixian. He knew all about birth and death, gain and loss of wealth, long and short life, and he predicted events with great accuracy. People held him in great awe.

One day Liezi, a person seeking the Tao, met Zixian and was fascinated by him. He went to Empty Gourd, the Taoist sage, and asked about Jixian. Previously he had thought that Empty Gourd was the best master, but now he wanted to learn the skills of the spirit medium Jixian.

Liezi had studied with Empty Gourd but had not put into practice his teachings of emptiness. He was like a chicken pecking at grain in a cage. No "master" rooster had yet been able to fertilize his eggs. Empty Gourd told Liezi to bring Jixian the medium to meet him.

The next day Liezi and Jixian went to visit Empty Gourd. When they arrived Empty Gourd was meditating on "earth" and "yin." Jixian did not know this, and thought that perhaps Empty Gourd was ill. The medium promised to heal him and return on the next day.

On the next day Empty Gourd was meditating on "yang"

and "heaven." All thoughts were emptied from his mind. He looked radiant and in good health. Jixian the medium said that it was due to his powers of healing that Empty Gourd looked better.

On the third day when Jixian came, Empty Gourd was meditating on taiji, with yin and yang in harmony (chapter 42 of the *Tao-te Ching*). Jixian had never seen such a meditation before and was puzzled.

On the fourth day Jixian came again to see Empty Gourd, who was sitting in forgetfulness, united with the Tao in the abyss of meditation.[18] Jixian fled and was never seen again. Empty Gourd urged Liezi to find him and bring him back. But Liezi never did find the spirit medium. Instead he learned the ways of emptying meditation, becoming "intoxicated" with inner peace.[19]

The way of the possessed medium and shaman trance is the polar opposite of the emptying meditations and "ecstasy" of Taoism. To confuse the two—mystic kenotic meditation with the shaman or medium trance—is to equate Jixian and Empty Gourd.

Liezi returned to his home and for three years did not go out. He cooked for his wife, and fed the pigs with the same respect as when banqueting humans. He got rid of all artifice and embraced simplicity. No matter what hardships and difficulties, he remained "one with Tao" to the end.

Wuwei Tao action is without fame or political schemes. It doesn't try to reform others or take away their special work. It is not a slave to knowledge. It uses its qi to heal, and is never exhausted. In a word, it is "empty" and thus always aware of Tao.

## Interior Peace

*Not reaching out, not holding on,*
*Responding, but not storing inside.*
*Thus he can overcome self and not harm others.*

Chuang-tzu ends the Inner Chapters with a final story:

*The lord of the southern ocean was bright [yang].*
*The lord of the northern ocean was obscure [yin].*
*The lord of the center was Hundun,*
*[primordial breath, taiji, emptiness].*
*Yang and Yin loved to go meet at Hundun's place,*
*Because Hundun treated them so nicely.*
*Yang and Yin thought they should do something for Hundun,*
*To thank him for his kindness.*
*"All humans have seven apertures,*
*So they can see, hear, eat, and rest.*
*Only Hundun doesn't have any.*
*Let's try to drill some for him."*
*So each day they drilled one opening [two eyes, ears,*
  *nostrils, a mouth].*
*On the seventh day Hundun died.*

So too the life of Tao's interior presence dies when we open the heart-mind to the thoughts, worries, and cares of the external world. The practice of sitting in forgetfulness and fasting in the heart made Hundun (huntun) alive to Tao's presence. Opening the seven apertures made Hundun's awareness end. The emptying of the mind and heart of all judgment, and the maintaining of peace and equilibrium, is the key to keeping the healing powers of Tao present. The meditation of the Taoist Lady Wei Huacun for emptying the heart-mind does just this.

✺ Chapter Three

# Centering Meditation; Colors That Heal

When the novice comes to the Taoist master to learn the meditations of healing, he or she is at first treated rather coldly and even turned away. Both Zen (Chan) Buddhists and traditional Taoist masters thus test the sincerity and humility of the applicant. Those who pass this first hurdle are told to read and put into practice the writings of Lao-tzu and Chuang-tzu, the meditations of the two mystics described in chapter 2. They are taught the way of nonjudgment that shuns worldly fame and glory. They are also encouraged to follow the rule (*jie*) of the Taoist way of life, not to seek wealth, fame, or power from the way of healing meditation about to be taught to them. Finally, they are urged to master the yin-yang five phase system (also called the five stages, movers, or elements), an ancient protoscientific way of classifying changes in nature. This age-old method of classifying nature's permutations relates to changes that take place in the human body (microcosm) as well as the outer world (macrocosm).

The five phase system developed quite naturally from patterns observed in the yin-yang cycles of nature. Thus, as Lao-tzu's forty-second chapter explained, Tao gave birth to One (primordial breath). One in moving gave birth to Two (yang), and resting produced Three (yin). Another view of the process taught that One breath gave birth to the two principles of life, yin and yang. Joining, yang and yin formed the visible world. Separating, yang (fire) went upward to form the heavens while yin (water) flowed downward to fill the world beneath earth in the ocean. Heaven, earth, and water or underworld were thus born of yin and yang. The two principles continuously generate the three realms.

The two principles also inform the four seasons and the visible world of nature. Yang produces spring and summer, while yin brings forth autumn and winter. Yang dominates from sunrise through the early afternoon, while yin rules from sunset through sunrise. In living things yang governs birth to maturity while yin prevails from later maturity through old age. Thus the two principles born from primordial energy, yang (male, bright, active, moving, ascending, fire, destroying) and yin (female, obscure, passive, resting, descending, water, birthing, and nourishing) are at work in all of the myriad creatures gestated from Tao.

The four seasons are spatially related to the five directions. Spring corresponds to the east, the color blue-green, and the element wood. Summer is in harmony with the south, the color red, and the element fire. Autumn responds to the west, the color white (the silvery sun shining on ripening wheat in the late afternoon), and the element metal (the scythe used to cut the autumn harvest). Winter touches the north, the deep

## Centering Meditation; Colors That Heal

purple of the sky before dawn, and the element water. A fifth referent is added in the Chinese system, the place of humans standing in the center of the cosmos watching the process of change going on in the world around. For the meditating Taoist, the center is celebrated in Chinese festivals during the third, sixth, ninth, and twelfth lunar months. Its color is a bright gold-yellow, its element is earth, and its function is to heal.

Thus there are five phases or elements in the Chinese system, each with its own season, color, musical tone, and spatial and temporal referent in the outer cosmos, and a storing place within the body. The five elemental phases are related to the inner and outer cosmos as follows:

| Phase | Time | Color/Aura | Space | Organ | Symbol | Rite | Tone (note) |
|---|---|---|---|---|---|---|---|
| wood | spring | blue-green | east | liver | dragon | birth | jiao (mi) |
| fire | summer | bright red | south | heart | phoenix | grow | zhi (sol) |
| metal | autumn | white | west | lungs | tiger | marry | gong (do) |
| water | winter | dark purple | north | kidneys | turtle | aging | shang (re) |
| earth | third, sixth, ninth, twelfth months | gold-yellow | center | spleen | kiln | renew | yü (la) |

The human body and its vital organs are intimately bound together with the outer world of nature and its cyclical changes. To be in tune with these changes is an essential part of well-being. Spring and the nourishing color of bright green resonate in the liver. Summer and the warm ripening color of red reside in the heart. Autumn and the maturing color of silver or white dwell in the lungs. Winter and the deep generating color of purple are found in the kidneys. The central organ where the bright healing yellow of earth is stored is the spleen. These five organs, the liver, heart, lungs, kidneys, and spleen, are called *zang* (*tsang*) or "storing" places, because the elements of birthing, growing, maturation, harvest, and rest-generation are stored there.

Another set of organs in the lower part of the body are called *fu* or passages, because the oxygen, foods, and liquids brought into the body to nourish it pass through them. These are the stomach, the large and small intestines, the gallbladder, the urinary bladder, and a special term in Chinese traditional healing called the *sanjiao*, the three visceral channels (literally, three energy sources or heaters) bringing food, liquid, and oxygen-breath nourishment into the bloodstream and the whole body. The five *zang* store healing energy while the six *fu* process it. Even though all of the bodily organs are important in maintaining health, the five storage areas are particularly emphasized in the meditations of Taoist healing. This is because of the interrelationship between the "storage" areas and all the other organs. The inner and outer cosmos are related through meditating on these five organs. All of the healthy memories, colors, sounds, fragrances, or feelings that are stored in the human body evoke well-being in an orderly manner, through the passage of time and the cyclical changes of the seasons.

Thus the color of newly sprouting bright green grass, the leaves of a tree in spring, the deep green of an emerald, sun shining through pines on a moss-covered rock, are examples of color energy stored in the liver that can heal the human spirit. Bright red and pink roses, white star-burst chrysanthemums, deep blue-purple orchids, the golden yellows of marigolds and trumpet flowers, are used in decorative flower arrangements (in Western as well as in Chinese and Japanese flower art exhibits) for their intense aesthetic beauty. The Taoist uses the visualization of these colors, storing them in the five zang organs to heal inner stress, anxiety, and sorrow.

The same colors when seen in dull or sullied circumstances can also cause harm and illness. Dull green in dying plants cries to be uprooted and replanted. Dull red symbolizes anger, dull white means approaching death, dull blue brings sorrow ("I have the blues" is a common jazz musical statement), and dull yellow signals an overwhelming sense of negative judgment. Both the shaman and the Taoist systems of healing use the bright healing forms and avoid the dull negative variants of the color wavelength. The colors are interpreted in both systems as follows:

### Taoist (apophatic) and Shaman (kataphatic) Symbols

| Healing Colors | Harmful Colors |
|---|---|
| bright green (new life) | dull green (sickness) |
| bright red (love, brave) | dull red (anger, blood) |
| bright gold (healing, Buddha) | dull yellow (negative judgment) |
| bright white (salvation) | dull white (death) |
| bright blue, purple (prayer, peace) | dull blue (sad, trouble) |

The Taoist use of the colors listed in the left column is meditative, for instance, the envisioning of the color purple is thought to stimulate the pineal gland in the center of the brain, bringing about the excretion of the hormone melatonin to regenerate the body and bring good health. Meditating on bright purple, envisioning its energies circulating through the body and residing in the kidneys, brings health to these two lower organs and stimulates the ability of the mind to be creative.

(The meditation on breath circulation is explained on pages 81–83).

Bright green heals the liver, quells excessive fear or anxiety, and brings the energy of freshly growing spring grass to the body. Bright red such as found in roses or peonies changes anger to love, and fear to courage and changes the will (thought to reside in the heart) from selfishness to thoughts of generous giving. Thus humans are almost universally moved

*"The Five Color Breaths contemplate Tao." The five qi breaths (the children) are born from the five primordial elements. The Lingbao Five True Writs are held in the hands of the five spirits. Ch'ing dynasty woodblock print from Xingming Guizhi.*

## Centering Meditation; Colors That Heal

to send bright flowers to express feelings of love and giving. Fresh air conceived as bright white light is envisioned to be circulating through the body, clearing the lungs of polluting elements and the mind of festering thoughts and images. Bright gold-yellow heals the stomach and spleen of the ills caused by negative judgments and tensions.

Dull green is a sign of illness, dull blue of sadness, dull red of anger, dull yellow of negativity, and dull white of death. One of the most uncanny rites of Korean and Altaic shamans is the use of five flags—red, yellow, white, green, and blue—to diagnose illness and misfortune. Going into deep trance by rhythmic dance and drumming, the shaman travels into the netherworld and returns as a mythic general from the ancient past. The shaman holds five flags, colored bright red, bright yellow, white, dull green, and dull blue. The flags are wrapped into a bundle, and the sick person (or other onlookers) is invited to draw forth one of the staffs, not knowing which color will emerge. Drawing the dull blue flag means impending trouble, dull green means sickness, dull white means death (or the return of an ancestral spirit from the underworld to visit the living). Bright yellow is a symbol of the healing Buddha, and bright red means good fortune and blessing. Bright red or yellow change the three negative colors to well-being.

The meditation in which the five health-bringing colors are circulated through the body and stored in the five organs is taught by the Taoist master to only a few disciples. This is because the majority of those who come to study with the Taoist are interested in the medical, liturgical, or martial aspects of the Taoist arts as means to make a living rather than as steps toward mystical union with the Tao through emptying or kenosis. Many Westerners who come to study Taoism also miss the subtleties of Taoist ascesis in the pressure put on them to finish a doctoral dissertation or publish a learned article. All of these motives, whether for profit or reputation as a scholar, preclude the exercise of kenotic meditation. The Taoist master often remains silent or talks of other matters in the presence of martial artists and scholars.

Another powerful reason against teaching the method of color visualization to the novice who has not mastered the emptying way of Lao-tzu and Chuang-tzu is the fear that meditation of any sort, if not directed by a master, will lead to pride and selfish achievement for the misguided rather than a sense of selfless giving that is the sign of the person truly one with Tao's process. Thus the next step in the process of emptying through the use of color is a crucial one. It is also surprisingly simple and can be learned by children and the elderly in a few easy steps.

## CENTERING

The first step in the meditation is to be aware of the body's center of gravity. This is done by pointing to a place about two to three inches below the navel and then focusing attention on a spot two or more inches inside. This place is called the lower cinnabar field (*xia dantian, hsia tan-t'ian*) in Taoist terminology. The meditator is told to imagine it to be in front of the two kidneys, a kind of doorway to the body's physical and spiritual (mystical) center. In the Taoist system there are three such centers in the body. The first, called the upper cinnabar field (*shang dantian, shang tan-t'ian*) is in the center of the head, the region that in modern medicine would be called the pineal gland. This place is called the center of qi, one's mental energies, thought, imagination, judgment, concept, and other activities of the mind. The second center is called the middle or center cinnabar field (*zhong dantian, chung tan-t'ian*). It is the human heart or pericardial region, the center of yang, will, love, desire, hatred, and other willed attitudes toward external objects that follow on the conceptual judgment of the mind.

The third center, the lower cinnabar field, (*xia dantian*) is the true center of gravity in the body, the seat of yin, intuition, wisdom, and direct awareness of reality that is not mediated by intellectual judgment or will. The intellect and will are human faculties whose object is the outer world of change and impermanence. The belly's intuition alone is able to be aware of the transcendent, unmoving, eternal Tao.

Thus in Taoist philosophy and spirituality (the two are the same) the intellect and the will are used solely to understand the changes that take place in nature. The intellect names, defines, and judges the myriad things gestated by qi, yang, and yin. The will freely (sometimes arbitrarily) chooses or rejects according to the judgments of the mind, as for instance, whether a thing brings fame, power, or wealth to the person judging. Only by emptying the mind of concepts and the will of desires can the intuitive powers of the belly be actuated. The meditation of centering on the lower cinnabar field therefore actuates the human powers of intuition and wisdom.

These three human powers of intellect, will, and intuition are, like the five elements, intimately bound to the outer world of nature.

| intellect | idea | judgment | qi | breath | heaven | head |
| will | love | choice | shen | yang | earth | chest |
| intuition | wisdom | feeling | jing | yin | water | belly |

The intellect controls qi breath and can send it anywhere in the outer cosmos, just by thinking or projecting. Thus when one thinks of a distant place, one's mind goes there and imagines what it looks like. The mind can wander into the far-off heavens creating images of "star wars" or into a nine-tiered hell to see visions of punishment. The mind can also affect the body. When one is praised, mental images of glory and fame make the whole body feel elated. When scolded or blamed, fearful images remain in the mind and fester, harming and depressing the qi energies of the entire body. By emptying the images from the mind, whether of the outer cosmos or the world of social intercourse, qi energies are not dissipated either in over-elation or over-depression.

The spiritual energy in one's heart is like a king that rules over and controls the entire body. The *shen* or spiritual energy within is manifest in the human power of will. This inner ruler, whom Taoists envision as a king or queen dressed in red robes, is changed by meditation from a sophisticated self-willed potentate into a ruddy child. Nothing can harm the will that is childlike. As described in the meditations of Lao-tzu, tigers do not claw, serpents bite, or harmful spirits attack the "hierophant" infant in one's heart.

> How keep body and mind one?
> Be like a child.
> Be aware of breathing, be soft and pliant.
> To see the transcendent Tao, have a pure mind, . . .

## Centering Meditation; Colors That Heal

*Don't say no.*
*To receive heaven's blessing,*
*Be empty like a mother's womb,*
*Give birth and nurture, then let go.*

The meditation that focuses on the lower cinnabar field awakens intuitive awareness of the Tao while emptying the mind of image and judgment and making the will simple like a child. This state is brought about by focusing the attention on the centering spot that is two to three inches behind and below the navel, and then filling the body's organs with the five healing colors.

*Color blinds the eye, sound deafens the ear.*
*Flavor dulls the taste, . . .*
*The Taoist sage fills the belly, not the eyes.*
*Value what is inside, not what is outside.*

The goal of the Taoist color meditation, as with Taoist music and visualization, is precisely to fill the mind with color and the ears with sound that dull the senses and the imagination to the worries, cares, and selfish goals of the exterior world. The mind saturated in healing colors, the ears with healing music, and the imagination with sacred images is easily urged on to the next step of total kenosis emptiness, and immersion in the Tao.[1]

Instruction begins with a meditation that focuses on the circulation of breath. The student is told to fill the lungs with air by breathing in slowly through the nose and exhaling quietly through the mouth. If the nose is stuffy and breathing seems difficult, the master shows how, by focusing attention on the lower throat and esophagus instead of the nostrils, the air flows in more freely. The breathing process is extended so that one breathes air into the lungs for about thirty seconds, pauses briefly, and then exhales quietly though the mouth for another thirty seconds.

In the classical Taoist system, unlike other forms of breathing yoga, inhalation and exhalation are done without any audible sound. This is because awareness is extended to every slightest sound, including the passing of vehicles outside, the singing of birds, barking of dogs, and crying of children at a great distance. As the meditation progresses, the sounds of an air-conditioner, of neon lights overhead, of refrigerators and ticking clocks, become almost unbearable. When performed correctly external and internal sounds are not drowned out but become more acute in Taoist and Buddhist centering meditation. These are signs that the meditation is being performed correctly.

Next the meditator is told to focus attention on the breath process within the body. Air breathed into the lungs flows into the bloodstream, and is pumped by the heart through the entire body. The meditator watches this process, how air circulates from the lungs into the blood, down the front side of the body to the tip of the toes, up the back side of the legs, the backbone, the neck to the top of the skull, and downward again along the front of the face to be breathed outward through the mouth. The efficacy of the meditation (the "secret" passed on orally by the master) is that one watches this process as if with one's eyes. One is told to follow the circulating breath with semi-closed eyes, moving the eyeballs first downward, then upward, following the breath energy as it goes down the front side (*ren*

## Centering Meditation; Colors That Heal

channel) and up the back side (*du* channel), following it up to the top of the skull, down the forehead and nose ridge, and out through the mouth.

In a subsequent lesson this process will be visualized as a marvelous stream of bright light or fresh water that washes through the body, leaning out past memories, aches, and blockages. The air (qi breath energy) can be made to flow through aching joints, cleansing and opening them to healing. But in this first lesson, the oxygen and revivifying energy in the bloodstream is simply envisioned to be flowing through the body, revitalizing it. The process of circulation should take about twenty-three to thirty seconds, the actual time it takes for blood to be pumped through the body and brought back to the lungs to expel carbon dioxide and receive more oxygen. The reason pure air is breathed in through the nostrils and sullied air is exhaled through the mouth is simply to help focus the mind on the process of circulation. The mind thus occupied is freed from worries and the heart from selfish desires.

This first meditation on breathing can be performed anywhere and in any position. One can practice it while sitting in a bus, a classroom, or a long-winded Sunday sermon. Those who cannot manage a full-lotus sitting position (both legs crossed with the bottoms of the feet upward) may sit in a half-lotus (one foot up) or simply cross-legged, as when watching a campfire. One can also practice the breathing meditation before getting out of bed in the morning, while lying down, reclining, or standing. The beautiful motions of tai chi chuan dance, when done properly, act out the circulating of breath energy through the body, bringing in energy, circulating it through the body, and sending it outward.[2] The most important thing to keep in mind in any of the Taoist meditations is the rule to remain natural and comfortable. That which puts strain on the body, causing discomfort or distress, cannot be practiced for any great length of time. Like walking on tiptoe, in a strong wind or violent rain, nature does not allow the human body to tolerate pain or distress for long.[3]

> *Violent winds last only a morning,*
> *A great rainfall is over in a day.*
> *Heaven and earth make sure . . .*
> *Violence does not endure.*

The second step in learning the meditation of healing color is to focus attention on the lower cinnabar field, the center of gravity below the solar plexus in the human body. This second step in Taoist meditation is done without reference to breathing, for the moment. The meditator assumes a comfortable sitting position, perhaps by putting a cushion or pillow on the floor and sitting on the cushion cross-legged. As in the first step of the meditation, a chair, bench, or couch may also be used, whatever is at hand and comfortable. The hands may be folded in the lap, so that they are held directly in front and slightly below the navel, thus keeping the meditator aware of the place for focusing attention.[4] While in this position the attention is focused on a point two to three inches below the navel and two to three inches within, depending on the size and weight of the meditator. To become aware of this fulcrum or center of gravity in the body is the point of the meditation. Artists, athletes, truck drivers, cyclists, musicians, poets, and writers are said to be unconsciously aware of this intuitive focus when acting in their professional capacity. Thus a basketball

## Centering Meditation; Colors That Heal

star shooting a basket, an artist's brush stroke, the "golden section" in nature, are examples of centering focus.[5]

An easy way to find the body's center when sitting on a cushion is to place the palm of the hand just below the navel and rock back and forth. The center of the hand will be located on the pivot, the place that moves the least when rocking back and forth. Imagine a spot within the body behind the palm of the hand, about two or so inches inside. Consider this place to be the body's center of gravity. The meditation of centering focuses attention on this place. Taoist art conceives of it as a "void chamber" in the body's center.

The meditator, by focusing attention on this point, brings the qi mental energies of the mind down into the lower cinnabar field. It is from here that intuitive awareness of the inner and outer cosmos begins to takes place. Focusing the mind's attention on this place can be done as a process. One is first aware of the upper cinnabar field, that is, the very center of the human brain where the pineal gland is envisioned to be. The meditator is helped by imagining this place to be filled with a bright purple flame, which is made to move downward from the center of the brain to the throat, the pericardial region (the heart), lungs, belly, and finally come to rest in the lower cinnabar field. Thus, like an elevator moving from an upper floor to the basement, the mind is seen to be lowered into the belly and allowed to rest there, from which place it looks outward at reality.[6]

Once that awareness of the external world is felt in the belly, the meditator can be compared to a diver with goggles who looks up at the surface of the water, watching things float by. The things floating on the surface of the mind far above, such as ideas, concepts, images, are like flotsam and jetsam drifting on the surface of the sea. The meditator no longer grasps on to these distant ideas but lets them drift away, out of reach of the mind peacefully at rest in the belly.

Once the meditator has become adept at bringing the mind to rest in the lower cinnabar field, he or she may also envision the middle cinnabar field, the heart, with its red-robed ruler, the "human will" spirit, residing there. The heart spirit is seen to be enveloped in a red light. It too is led down by the imagination into the lower cinnabar field. Here it changes from an imperious ruler to a reddish pink-clad infant. Now the intellect and its qi energy and the heart with its willful shen spirit are both resting peacefully in the belly. At this point in the meditation the beginner is simply told to be aware of the centering place in the belly, and to look outward from this vantage point at the external world.[7]

Meditation may be an entirely new experience for many who read about Taoist visualization techniques for the first time. The notion of awareness of the outside world from the body's physical center may be an unfamiliar idea. It is useful to pause and reflect on its significance. Scientists debate the objectivity of intuitive feelings and the "sixth sense" in the realm of scientific investigation. There is certainly a universal awareness of intuitive perception. No culture or religious system can be said to have a monopoly on intuition, just as no language can be said to have a monopoly on logic.[8] Whatever scientific arguments are used for or against intuition, the point of the centering meditation is simply to make the novice intensely aware of what is going on in the world outside the self without being impeded by mental distractions or willful desires. The Taoist and Buddhist centering experience demonstrates that intuition alone, perception that does not rely on words for its comprehension, can make the meditator aware of transcendent or nonchanging presence. Peace of mind and heart are brought about by focusing on the permanent, nonchanging aspects of reality. It is this taste that is savored in the first experience of the quiet intuitive center in the lower belly area.[9]

A much simpler way of "meditating from the belly" (the lower cinnabar field) is simply to focus indirect attention on the area two to three inches below the navel and two to three inches within. This simple form of physical awareness can be done while driving a car, riding a bus, sitting in a church, temple, or shrine, listening to a lecture, or doing any other activity, such as walking, swimming, or playing sports. The effect on the physical body is to give a sense of quiet well-being that remains unruffled in the presence of internal stress or external excitement. Focusing indirect attention on the lower peritoneal (solar plexus) area quiets the action of the mind, balances the will and judgment, and calms the nerves by taking attention away from mind-imposed images and worries. Whenever attention is focused in the belly, either directly or indirectly, worries in the mind and unfulfilled desires in the heart almost immediately cease to drain the body's physical and mental energy.

The realization that thoughts created in one's mind exist only in one's mind (certainly in no one else's) is a rare insight to be cherished deeply. All mental thoughts and images are like leeches that suck blood and energy only as long as one leaves them there to do so. Peace of mind means in fact an understanding freed from any form of lingering judgment and unforgiven offenses. The peace that ensues from this freedom heals the self from a myriad festering memories and begins the healing process.

Getting rid of lingering images that recall stress and anxiety is one of the first goals of the centering meditation. Once the mind is cleared and the heart freed from all manner of worries, then the belly's intuitive awareness of the inner and outer world become far more desirable than the former condition of constant worry about deadlines, homework, schedules, failures, and what others are thinking or saying about one. With the mind and heart quieted, and the pressure to "do" and to "finish" work relieved, the same work is in fact accomplished far more efficiently.[10]

> *Be happy when scolded,*
> *Fearful when praised.*
> *By the very fact that this body is alive,*
> *Difficulties and contradictions come to us.*
> *If we were dead, disasters wouldn't occur.*
> *So value difficulties, if you value your life.*
> *Only when we forget selfish interests*
> *Can we be entrusted with ruling the world.*

Acquiring the ability to disregard bickering, scoldings, and unjust accusations is not as difficult as overcoming the desire for praise, fame, and the power ensuing from human acclaim and approval. In the teachings of Lao-tzu and Chuang-tzu, praise and glory are far more dangerous to well-being than disrespect, scoldings, or blame. To transcend all forms of mental illusions, whether from personal or social sources, is to heal (make whole)

## Centering Meditation; Colors That Heal

much of the illness arising from within the human heart and mind.

The emptying of the mind of worry and self-illusion is achieved by the meditation of centering. The teachings of Chuang-tzu on *xinzhai* heart fasting and *zuowang* sitting in forgetfulness are put into practice by this simple technique. When attention is focused on the belly the mind becomes like a mirror, which does not store up images but simply reflects and lets go:

> *The person who has touched Tao*
> *Uses the heart like a mirror*
> *Not reaching out, not holding on,*
> *Responding, but not storing inside.*
> *Thus he can overcome self and not harm others.*[11]

The meditation that empties heart and mind makes the meditator "touch" or be one with the transcendent Tao. In the words of Chuang-tzu, "*Wei dao ji xu*," Only Tao dwells in the void [center]. In such a state of quiet centering, the meditator can see and respond to the needs of those around without exhausting his or her own source of qi energy, and can thus heal rather than harm others.

The teachings of Lao-tzu and Chuang-tzu summarized in chapter 2 are now even more meaningful to the meditator who has achieved sitting in forgetfulness and heart fasting. The intensification of awareness of nature's changes around the meditator makes the very experience of wind, rain, sky, thunder, stars, sunrise, and sunset far more important than watching evening television or following the human tragedies exploited in the daily press. The traditional Taoist master who teaches meditation gives up any form of exterior distraction, including movies, television, newspapers, novels, lectures, and conferences, to maintain this sense of peace and unity with the transcendent Tao hidden behind and gestating and nourishing the changes seen in nature. The meditator is told to "listen to the quiet intervals in between the rustling of leaves and the song of the wind." Like the quiet between breaking waves and the sky at dawn and sunset, nature's most beautiful sounds and colors are found by listening to the "flute of heaven [Tao]" that is heard in quiet stillness.[12]

The meditation of awareness of Tao's presence within the lower cinnabar field, the centering meditation beneath the solar plexus, soon becomes an almost continuous form of meditative awareness for the practitioner. Friends comment on the new sense of peace found in the person who practices this meditation. Worries about livelihood, reputation, glory, and success are lessened and eventually extinguished. The joy of centering meditation removes the need for other kinds of gratification. The "high" achieved by certain kinds of drugs and alcohol, the straining need for addictive substances, are obstacles to peace and awareness.[13]

## Storing Colors in the Five Organs

Once the centering meditation has been learned, the novice is led by the master into the world of color visualization and storing. There are many ways of visualizing colors. The easiest way is to have a bouquet of flowers nearby, or a garden outside the window. A deep forest in the mountains, the

## Centering Meditation; Colors That Heal

seashore at sunrise or sunset, or one's own room are all good places for meditation. Some people have strong imaginations and can visualize a color as soon as the meditation teacher names it. Others need to have the color nearby to see it concretely before visualizing and circulating it meditatively through the body. It is best to buy bright flowers or artistic pictures with bright colors, and have these at hand when doing the meditation for the first time. Once accustomed to the meditation it can be done anywhere without the need for art or nature as an aid.[14]

The colors are chosen according to the time of the year, month, day, and hour of the meditation. The choice approximates the following chart:

| Color | Time | Image | Season | Lunar Months | Body | Tone | Direction |
|---|---|---|---|---|---|---|---|
| green | 7–11 A.M. | grass | spring | first, second | liver | C# | east |
| red | 1–3 P.M. | rose | summer | fourth, fifth | heart | D# | south |
| white | 3–5 P.M. | sun | autumn | seventh, eighth | lungs | F# | west |
| violet | 7–9 P.M. | purple orchid | winter | tenth, eleventh | kidneys | G# | north |
| gold | noon, midnight, sunrise, sunset | gold |  | third, sixth, ninth twelfth | spleen | A# | center |

The time of the day, month, direction, and musical note evoke the color and healing power of the corresponding element.[15] For the novice learning the meditation for the first time, seeing the colors and circulating them through the body are key steps in learning the healing process. Each color has a specific healing role. The meditation is taught as follows:

**Meditation on bright green.** Choose a comfortable place to sit quietly, free from drafts and distracting noises. One may sit cross-legged on a cushion, on a chair, by the seashore, in a mountain forest, or on a park bench, wherever one pleases. Begin the meditation by centering, as taught earlier in this chapter. When the mind and heart are freed from distractions, envision or look at a bright green color directly in the foreground of your attention. See this green color to be refreshing like green grass in spring, light reflecting from moss in a deep forest, the bright green of an emerald, or the refreshing fragrance of pine needles. Breathe in this green through the nostrils, and see the color circulate through the body like a renewing aroma. Follow the bright green color with the eyes of the imagination as it circulates through the body. Bring it down to the toes and up the backbone, over the top of the head and down to the mouth. From there exhale the breath quietly, and again use the imagination to examine the exhaled breath to see if it is a pure bright green, or if it has been sullied by picking up worries, cares, and unhealthy elements as it passed through the body.[16]

Repeat the meditation several times, until a bright green color is envisioned when the breath is expelled. Bright green represents the restoring powers of spring that revivify and refresh the body's energies. During this process whatever cares or worries may have remained after the first step of centering are further cleansed.

When the meditator can visualize a pure bright green color, the conclusion of the meditation takes place. The purified green color is imagined in front of the meditator. It is breathed into the body and stored in the liver. The meditator must see in the eyes of the imagination the liver as being on the right side of the body, just below the rib cage. To assist the meditation, the Taoist presses the tip of the thumb of the left hand to the middle joint of the index finger on the left hand. This mudra is used to store the revivifying green color in the liver and recall it for healing whenever the healing of cares, worries, or anxiety is needed.[17]

The color green can henceforth be used to renew the body when tired. Sitting on a green lawn, walking through a pine forest, seeing moss growing on stones, are all occasions when healing green can be stored in the liver. After a tiring lecture, a day at the office, or a drive on a busy highway, the simple act of walking on a green lawn or listening to the leaves of trees stimulates the body to a sense of restored vitality and wholeness.

**Meditation on bright pink or red.** Sitting again in a favorite meditation spot, feel your awareness focus on the centering position. Imagine a warm, caring color of bright pink or red that is a sign of love or affection. This can easily be done by either imagining or having a freshly blossoming pink-red rose in front of you. With the eyes of the imagination see this bright pink-red color fill a sphere directly in front of you. Breath the bright red color into the body through the nose and see it circulate through the entire body as described in the meditation on green. The bright red color cleans the entire body of any resident feelings of anger, frustration, and vengeance. Breathe the color out through the mouth, and repeat the meditation several times, until any vestiges of anger, unfulfilled desires, and indignation are removed.

When the bright pink-red color dominates the consciousness and fills the interior with a sense of benevolence, then with the eyes of the imagination see it to be poured into the heart and stored there. To assist in this process, the Taoist presses the tip of the thumb of the left hand to the tip of the middle finger, a mudra or hand symbol linking the season summer, the direction south, the element fire, and the heart together into a single meditative unit. Henceforth the color pink can be summoned from the heart by using this mudra to quell anger, opposition, and concupiscence. The pink-red color can be evoked to arouse a sense of benevolence within oneself and in others.[18]

**Meditation on bright white.** The color bright white, seen as rays from the afternoon sun, purifies the lungs and the entire body of any sullying images from the realm of sensuality, greed, and corruption. The bright white light breathed into the body in this meditation sees through artifice, deception, and pretense, totally emptying the mind of any trace of selfish power, desire for fame, or aggrandizement. Healing is effective only when motives are pure and selfless.

When sitting in a favorite meditation place, envision the bright white rays of the afternoon sun as enveloping the body.[19] First become aware of the body's focal center, and then breathe the bright white rays of the sun into the body through the nose. See them circulate everywhere, cleansing the body of aches and pains, purifying the mind of selfish thoughts and impure motives. When doing this meditation, those who smoke often see the lungs filled with the tar stains of tobacco, while those whose minds are filled with worries see blockages and dark obstacles as the bright light passes through the upper part of the body or the top of the head. Worries and stains are breathed out through the mouth. Perform the meditation several times, until the imagination sees the bright white light breathed out of the mouth to be pure and unsullied.

The meditator then breathes the white light of the sun into

## Centering Meditation; Colors That Heal

the lungs and stores it there while pressing the thumb of the left hand to the middle joint of the ring finger on the left hand. This mudra or hand symbol, which presses the thumb to the ring finger, touches the meditative meridian or connecting point between the lungs, the west, the season of autumn, and the element metal. The element metal can be envisioned as a bright silver sword that cuts away all selfishness, pretense, and fraudulent ideas from the mind and protects the body from evil. On the sword are inscribed the seven stars of the Big Dipper, Ursa Major, the constellation in the northern heavens that always points to true north. The Big Dipper is the symbol and model of Taoist practice, keeping the meditator's mind, heart, and belly always focused on the Tao in the center. Henceforth the color white is invoked to purify the mind, will, and senses.

**Meditation on bright purple.** The color purple brings health to the kidneys, renews the creative process within the mind, and leads to a sense of deep peace (the alpha state) during meditation.[20] Some Taoist masters (of Dragon-Tiger Mountain in Jiangxi Province and Mao Shan near Nanjing) immediately visualize the color purple emanating from the upper cinnabar field, the pineal gland area, when performing the centering meditation. An orchid, morning glory, or some other flower of a deep purple-blue tone can be used to assist the beginner to visualize the color purple.

The meditator sees the color purple diffuse throughout the body, bringing feelings of peace, relaxation, and refreshing re-creation to the entire person. This meditation can be performed before an important examination or interview, to arouse a sense of creativity and intuitive insight. When the purple aura has purified the mind, heart, and senses, it is stored in the kidneys.

The meditator presses the tip of the left thumb to the base of the third or middle finger (at the spot where the finger joins the hand). This meridian connects the kidneys to the direction north, the element water, and the season winter.

**Meditation on healing gold-yellow.** The last of the healing color meditations suffuses the person meditating in a bright gold-yellow. The color of bright yellow is the most important meditative color, since it changes negative feelings of the body, judgments of the mind, and worries of the heart into positive healing powers.[21] The meditator may envision a bright yellow flower or a glowing gold-yellow light that surrounds the person meditating and is breathed in through the nose and diffused throughout the body. Any negative colors such as dull yellow (negative judgments) or dull green (pain or illness) are washed away as the gold color flows through the arteries and veins. The meditation can be repeated several times, until a bright gold-yellow dominates the imagination. The meditator presses the middle joint of the third finger on the left hand with the tip of the left thumb and stores the gold color in the spleen when the meditation is concluded.

For those who cannot easily control the imagination or visualization of this or any of the above colors, it suffices to be aware of the bright yellow of a flower or the polished gold of a statue, a piece of art, or jewelry to perform the meditation. Followers of religions that censure the use of statues and images can perform the meditation by contemplating sacred words or geometric patterns, as in the religious art of Islam. Buddhism in its Theravada, Mahayana, and Tantric forms makes use of gold in most sacred images. A rich source of color visualization can be found in all religious and cultural traditions.[22]

## Centering Meditation; Colors That Heal

❈

Meditating on the five colors is analogous to contemplating the five spirits of the seasons, directions, musical notes (sound), fragrances, tastes, and bodily organs. The Taoist priest and Tantric Buddhist monk perform these meditations in a more elaborate manner. The five directions are envisioned to be a grand mandala or geometric design of a centered cosmos. In each of the five directions, in the many squares or circles of the mandala, and in each corresponding organ of the human body the meditator envisions a spirit to reside. The spirit is envisioned in exact detail. It is then meditatively "changed" into a sacred symbol such as a Sanskrit word or a flower, then into a color. Finally it is burned or washed away in the meditator's imagination so that nothing is left. This process is described more fully in chapter 4, the interpretative translation of the *Gold Pavilion* classic.

The layperson need not envision the spirits in the same detail required of the Taoist or the Tibetan Tantric monk. The process of seeing and storing the colors in the body is sufficient to bring about the quelling of mental judgment and inordinate desires. The meditations of emptying described in chapter 4 are as easy to practice as those described here. Though the text of the *Gold Pavilion* classic is complicated (the text is kept deliberately obscure, elliptical, sometimes even repetitive), the method itself is simple. The commentary immediately following each passage shows that behind the complicated system of symbols the method is indeed quite easy to follow, even for persons other than a Taoist priest or monk. Purity of mind and heart, the ascetics of Lao-tzu and Chuang-tzu, are the only requirements of the person who would proceed further.

## CHAPTER FOUR

# THE GOLD PAVILION CLASSIC; TAOIST EMPTYING MEDITATION

The text of the *Gold Pavilion* classic is found in the numbered lines, followed by line-by-line commentary that explains the cryptic meaning of the text. See the glossary for a list of terms.

## I

*First Stanza* (Lines 1–7)

1 Lao-tzu, dwelling alone, made these seven word refrains,
2 To cast off body and all spirit form.
3 Above is Gold Pavilion, below primordial pass;
4 Behind the *yu-chüeh* dark palace; in front of the gate of life.
5 Breathe in and out, between grass hut and cinnabar field;
6 Jade pool pure water, poured on spirit root.
7 All who can perfect this, constantly meditate [on Tao present].

**LINE 1** To dwell alone means to void mind and heart of worries, judgments, and images.

## The Gold Pavilion

❊

**LINE 2** The purpose of the *Gold Pavilion* classic is to teach the meditator to cast off all attachment to bodily form, and all of the spirits or spiritual forces that dwell in the microcosm, thus creating inner peace and emptiness.

**LINE 3** The Gold Pavilion is a "void space" above the kidneys, in the body's focal point, the physical center of gravity. It is the void center of the body's microcosm, from whence the Tao gestates the One breath; Two yang; and Three yin, as in the *Tao-te Ching*, chapter 42.

The One is breath or *ch'i*, which governs intellect, thought, in the upper cinnabar field, the head. The Two is yang or *shen* soul, which rules as king of the body, the power of will, in the central cinnabar field, the heart. The Three is yin, the power of intuition *ching*, which is located in the lower cinnabar field approximately two inches below the navel and three inches within, directly in front of the kidneys. Primordial pass, *kuan-yüan*, is a specific point used in acupuncture, referring to the external access point that gives entrance to the lower cinnabar field, the "ocean of breath." The *kuan-yüan* or primordial pass is the entrance to the Gold Pavilion, where the mind focuses or concentrates attention on the transcendent Tao during the meditation.

**LINE 4** The *yu-chüeh* acupuncture point is below the navel, through which the two kidneys can be accessed. The *mingmen* gate of life is an acupuncture point on the back, in front of which the primordial pass and the kidneys are located. The interior *yu-chüeh* dark palace, the gateway to the Gold Pavilion and Tao's presence within the body, is located between the two kidneys, midway between front and back. The acupuncture points

# The Gold Pavilion Classic; Taoist Emptying Meditation

❊

guide the meditator to the places where the mind focuses during meditation.

**LINE 5** The grass hut for inhaling and exhaling refers to the lungs. Air drawn into the lungs is visualized to circulate from the lungs and pericardial region (the area surrounding the heart) down to the lower cinnabar field and back up again. The heart is the organ identified with fire and heat purgation, while the kidneys are the source of coolness and water purification. The *ch'i* is seen to circulate within this furnace, pumped in a circular motion by the bellows of the lungs. The meditation burns, washes away, and purifies all thoughts and desires, and all spiritual images, before the intuitive audience with the Tao in the Gold Pavilion can be experienced.

**LINE 6** The term *jade pool* has two meanings: the throat, down which saliva is swallowed to be mixed with breath in the belly; and the two kidneys, in which the ch'i, first purged by the heart's fire, is now purified by the waters of the kidney. Once purified by fire and water, the mind's ch'i, heart's will, and belly's intuition are poured into the Gold Pavilion, to be nourished by awareness of Tao's presence.

**LINE 7** All, men and women alike, who are able to practice this method can attain a constant awareness of Tao's gestating presence within, giving birth to the "One, Two, Three . . . ," as in the forty-second chapter of the *Tao te Ching*. The word *ts'un*, or "meditate" can also be translated as to exist, to keep.

## Second Stanza (lines 8–13)

8  The human in the center pavilion dressed in clothes of red,

*The Gold Pavilion*

9  Closes and bolts the double doors of the Gold Pavilion gates.
10 The dark pavilion is the entrance [to the Gold Pavilion] towering above,
11 For ching [intuition] and ch'i breath purified in the lower cinnabar field.
12 The jade pool's [kidneys'] clear water ascends, made fertile [in the Gold Pavilion];
13 Spirit's source is strong and firm, till old age it never weakens.

**LINE 8** The red-robed person who enters the Gold Pavilion in meditation is the will, or the *shen* spirit, normally lodged in the heart, the body's middle cinnabar field. The color of the heart is red; it controls the element fire, the direction south, and the season summer.

**LINE 9** The will, once focused in the Gold Pavilion, closes the two gateways, the *hsüan* or male yang doorway, which allows breath to enter, and the *p'in* or female yin gate, which let's ch'i thoughts and ching intuition slip away. The will thus provides the key to lock the gates of the Gold Pavilion, keeping mind and intuitive awareness focused within on the Tao. The passage can have three references: the purely physical; the yogic discipline of holding one's breath; and the purely spiritual sense of focusing on the Tao. The Taoist Mao Shan Shang-ch'ing (Shangqing) tradition attributed to Lady Wei Huacun allows only the third, meditative sense, focusing attention on the Tao.

**LINE 10** The *yu-chüeh* dark gateway between the kidneys is here the place of meditative attention. The Gold Pavilion is seen to tower above this spot: the meditator looks upward in awe from the lower cinnabar field, seeing the ch'i breath and ching intuitive awareness first purified by heart's fire and

## The Gold Pavilion Classic; Taoist Emptying Meditation

kidney's water, then circulated upward to Tao's presence in the Gold Pavilion.

**LINE 11** In the middle of the lower cinnabar field (between the two kidneys, the center of gravity of the body) ch'i breath and ching awareness are refined.

**LINE 12** When the jade pool (two kidneys), with their pure water, refine the intuition, it ascends and is made fertile and life-bearing within the Gold Pavilion. The commentary expresses here the theory of ordinary and purified breath. When the mind's attention is focused on the exterior world (when the five senses expand outward to the exterior world of change, also called the *hou-t'ien* posterior heavens), then the breath is impure. When the five senses are closed to the exterior world and focused on the Gold Pavilion (the *hsien-t'ien* prior heavens where the Tao of non-change dwells), then breath is purified. Breath and intuition, now made aware of Tao's presence, do not flow away.

**LINE 13** The source or root of spiritual awareness, the ability to focus on Tao's presence, is strengthened and solidified by this meditation on the Gold Pavilion. The Gold Pavilion is the *t'ai-chi*, the void place within the microcosm of the body, where the *wuchi*, the *wuwei chih tao*, or the Tao of Transcendent Act, is present. The text states that this awareness does not weaken even in old age; the meditator focused on the Tao is in fact outside the world of change and thus does not age.

### Third Stanza (lines 14–19)

14 The central pond [heart] has a master who wears crimson clothes;

## The Gold Pavilion

15 Three inches below this field is where the shen spirit dwells.
16 Link to the outer and inner worlds, repeatedly disconnect them;
17 The center of the spirit's dwelling must be kept in order [free of judgment].
18 The upper chest, ch'i breath's passage, is intuition's *fu* tally;
19 Quickly strengthen ching awareness, then of itself attention is focused.

**LINE 14** The central pond is the pericardial region, or the middle cinnabar field. The shen spirit rules over the body as "will" from this region. Red clothing signifies that the heart rules over the element fire, the direction south, and the season summer.

**LINE 15** The shen soul-spirit resides three inches below the top of the pericardial area, below the acupuncture point where the third rib bones join in the center of the chest: the middle cinnabar field.

**LINE 16** The role of the shen spirit in the meditation is to keep the five senses (sight, smell, hearing, taste, touch) from rushing outward to focus on the judgments, thoughts, and desires of the outer world.

**LINE 17** The shen spirit's dwelling itself must be continually swept and kept clean from judgment, sensual attraction, fame, and glory, a teaching from the inner chapters of the Chuang-tzu.

**LINE 18** The *hsüan-ying* upper rib cage and the *ch'i-kuan* air pipes or conductors of breath (by mental attention) are here

# The Gold Pavilion Classic; Taoist Emptying Meditation

✦

personified. The spiritual forces governing these functions make a *fu* talismanic contract with the ching intuitive powers of the belly, to keep attention focused on the Tao.

**LINE 19** The very act of focusing attention on Tao's presence in the Gold Pavilion is so strengthening that the intuition holds on to the sense of transcendent awareness and does not allow itself to be drawn away.

*Fourth Stanza* (lines 20–23)
20  In the central hall there is a master, always dressed in red.
21  If you can envision him, sickness can be crushed.
22  From this center vertically, one foot up and down,
23  If you can circulate breath here, there will be no ill.

**LINE 20** The red-robed spirit within the heart purifies the depths of one's own nature. The heart that is at peace, freed from negative thoughts and judgments, preserves the entire body from illness.

**LINE 21** The red fires of the heart, through meditative vision, purify the body of all sickness and empty the mind of all negative thoughts. Healing (wholeness) and peace result from thus purifying the heart.

**LINE 22** The breath is circulated from the nose downward to the fires of the heart and then to the waters of the kidney. From there it is sent back upward again and expelled through the mouth. The elliptical circulation of breath is approximately a Chinese *ch'ih* foot in diameter.

**LINE 23** The man or woman who can guard the mind and

*The Gold Pavilion*

❂

heart from negative thoughts and selfish desires, by visualizing the circulation and purification of breath, thereby causes the entire body to be healthy. Illness is seen as a result of negative judgments, desires, and feelings. The meditation on circulating breath visually expels these evils.

*Fifth Stanza* (lines 24–29)

24 Breathing in and out within the [Gold] interior pavilion will renew the self;
25 By preserving constant inner ch'i focus, the body is filled with blessing.
26 Inside the *fang-ts'un* [Gold Pavilion], carefully cover and store ch'i.
27 Shen spirit and ching intuition returned there, though old, are made new.
28 Through the dark palace make them flow, down to the lower realm.
29 Nourish your jade tree, now a youth again.

**LINE 24** The focus is now changed to the lower cinnabar field and the entrance to the Gold Pavilion. Ch'i breath and ching awareness, once purified by fire and water, are restored to their primordial ageless condition.

**LINE 25** When breath (mind's attention) and ching (emotions, intuition) do not flow away after things in the world of change, the body does not age.

**LINE 26** Ch'i, the mind's attention, must remain centered in the Gold Pavilion. Centering, or "focusing on the belly," keeps ch'i from dissipating.

## The Gold Pavilion Classic; Taoist Emptying Meditation

❈

**LINE 27** The shen spirit or will, and the ching sense of intuitive awareness, alchemically refined by fire and water, are also renewed and sent into the Gold Pavilion. The man or woman who meditates thus becomes a child again. The Gold Pavilion is called *fang-ts'un* (square inch) here, indicating the spot two inches below the navel, three inches within, where the mind is focused.

**LINE 28** One visualizes ch'i, shen, and ching (intellect, will, and intuition) circulating down through the dark chamber between the kidneys into the Gold Pavilion.

**LINE 29** The term *jade tree* refers here to the sinews of primordial breath that run through the body and vivify it. When connected to the gestating power of the Tao within the Gold Pavilion, breath is restored to its primordial state. By nourishing primordial breath, the eternal youth within the self is renewed and the body made strong by Tao's gestating presence. The commentary rejects the way of sexual hygiene, calling it a lewd, non-Taoist practice.

*Sixth Stanza* (lines 30–34)

30 When Tao is touched, there is no disturbance, no confusion;
31 The *ling t'ai* [heart] meets heaven in the central field [Gold Pavilion].
32 From square inch [Gold Pavilion] center, down to the [dark] gate,
33 The soul's doorway to the Jade Chamber's [Gold Pavilion's] core is there.
34 All say that this is what thou, O Master, will teach us!

# The Gold Pavilion

❊

**LINE 30** From long ago until today, there has been only one pathway to the Tao: the way of peace and simplicity. The Tao is found without outwardly striving or inner confusion. Peace and simplicity must be found in both worlds, the invisible cosmos of the mind-spirit and the visible world touched by the body.

**LINE 31** The term *ling-t'ai*, spirit pavilion, means the heart. The central field is the Gold Pavilion, where the soul has audience with heaven, and Tao.

**LINE 32** Not only the soul-spirit but ch'i breath and ching intuition as well must enter the Gold Pavilion through the dark pass, as stated in line 10. The attention is now focused on this entrance.

**LINE 33** Again the teaching is repeated: the gateway to the Gold Pavilion and the Tao's presence is the dark chamber, the lower cinnabar field between the kidneys, the physical center of gravity of the body.

**LINE 34** The master of the method, Kung-tzu, is here interpreted to be the first of the Taoist trinity (San-ch'ing, the Three Pure Ones), Primordial Heavenly Worthy, Yüan-shih T'ien-tsun. Primordial Heavenly Worthy teaches that the Tao gestates and renews primordial breath from within the Gold Pavilion.

*Seventh Stanza* (lines 35–46)

35 The *ming-t'ang* [heart], in all four directions, is cleansed in ocean's depths,

36 Oh true [Tao-realized] person, a lone cinnabar sphere, see it here before you!

37 In the three passages, ching and ch'i are deep;

# The Gold Pavilion Classic; Taoist Emptying Meditation

38 If you desire long life, refine Mount K'un-lun.
39 The red palace layered tower has twelve stories;
40 Within its palace chambers the five breaths are stored.
41 The child of the red-walled city stands in the central pond.
42 Beneath it is a great wall, a mystery valley city.
43 The secrets of eternal birth, within this chamber are urgent.
44 Cast out all lewd immoral desires, only conserve ching essence.
45 The one-inch field in a foot-high cottage can then govern birth.
46 Forge the pill, constantly focus attention, heart kept at peace.

**LINE 35** The *ming-t'ang* bright palace was the structure used by the kings of early China and then by the emperor from the Han dynasty onward to sacrifice to the four seasons and five directions. Here it refers to the heart and the other four organs inside the body, which correspond as follows to the directions, elements, and seasons of the outer world:

| Organ | Direction | Season | Color | Element | Number | Symbol | Spirit |
|---|---|---|---|---|---|---|---|
| liver | east | spring | green | wood | 3 | dragon | Fu Hsi |
| heart | south | summer | red | fire | 2 | phoenix | Shen Nung |
| spleen | center | human | gold | earth | 5 | cauldron | Huang Ti |
| lungs | west | autumn | white | metal | 4 | tiger | Shao Hao |
| kidneys | north | winter | purple | water | 1 | tortoise | Chüan Hsü |

The term *hai-yüan* or ocean depths refers to the kidneys. Thus the heart and the other organs, the elements, directions, mind's thoughts, and heart's desires are all to be *fa*, governed or washed pure in the water of the kidneys before having audience with the Tao in the Gold Pavilion.

**LINE 36** The *chen-jen*, literally the "true" human, is a person who "sits in forgetfulness" and "fasts in the heart." Only Tao dwells within the center of the person who is empty, according to the *Chuang-tzu*, chapter 4. The "lone cinnabar sphere" refers to the center of the Gold Pavilion where a bright red drop of light, Tao gestating primordial breath, appears before the meditator.

**LINE 37** The term *san kuan*, three passes, has multiple meanings, depending on the interpretation given the passage. For the Taoist master it means the passages of ch'i breath, shen will, and ching intuition, sent inward to the Gold Pavilion or outward to the world of change. The text says that the three passages (in this case into the Gold Pavilion) are filled with ch'i breath, mind's focus, and ching intuition, belly's awareness. Mind controls the passage of ch'i from the upper cinnabar field, the pineal gland in the brain. Heart controls the passage of will-desire and the flow of words outward through the mouth and the hands to attain desires. The lower cinnabar field, the organs of the belly and the lower body, controls the outward flow of ching (emotional and intuitive awareness) and other fluids, wastes, and dispositions of the body. Intuitive awareness preserves ching within.

Note that the sexual hygiene school takes ching in the literal sense of semen, teaching that the male should not let semen flow away during intercourse, to nourish his own body instead with the retained semen. The female in turn is taught not to reach orgasm in order to "steal" the male essences and to preserve her own bodily fluids. Both the classical Taoist schools and reformed Ch'üan-chen Taoism reject all practice of

# The Gold Pavilion Classic; Taoist Emptying Meditation

sexual hygiene as non-Taoist, a form of selfish and self-centered practice unrelated to Lao-tzu or Chuang-tzu. If taken in the meditative rather than the physical sense, the three passages are conduits of ch'i breath awareness, shen will, and ching intuitive feelings inward to the Gold Pavilion or outward to be dissipated in search of fame, name, and possessions. The three outward paths are the nose and mouth for breath, the mouth and hands for will's desires, and the lower organs of the body for sensual gratification. The three inward passages are the brain center, the pineal gland (called Mount K'un-lun in the next line); the twelve stages of the spine (between the head and the heart) through which ch'i energy circulates; and the heart (pericardial area) itself. Note that access to the three passages through acupuncture are the *weilü* coccyx or sternum; the *hsia-chi* point on the upper spine; and the *yü-shen* on the back of the skull, access points to nourishing ching, shen, and ch'i.

**LINE 38** The person who desires to escape the dying process, to keep intuition, breath, and will from flowing away, must nourish and perfect Mount K'un-lun, the pineal gland in the brain's center, from which (in modern terms by melatonin and other hormones) the body's ch'i energy is nourished.

**LINE 39** Likewise such a person must focus on circulating breath from the center of the brain (Mount K'un-lun) downward to the heart and upward along the twelve points of the spine to the pineal gland, in a continually nourishing process.

**LINE 40** The five colors or vapors of the five elemental energies, that is, the green energy of spring from the liver, the summer red of the heart, the autumn white of the lungs, the

## The Gold Pavilion

dark winter of the kidneys, and the bright gold of the spleen are seen in meditative vision to be stored in the heart region. The tail of the Big Dipper revolving continuously in the heavens points to the direction from which the meditation (color visualization) begins. If the tail of the Big Dipper points east, then the meditator begins by bringing the color green from the liver into the heart region, and so forth in ordered succession (south, west, north, center).

LINE 41 The youthful spirit of the heart is like a child standing in the middle of a pool, bathed in the aura of the five colors.

LINE 42 "Beneath it is a great wall" refers to the *jen* (*ren*) passage of acupuncture points that pass down the front of the body from the chin to the toes, and the *tu* (*du*) passage that runs from the heels upward along the spine to the top of the head and back down to the nose, through which the colors are circulated. The city in the mysterious valley refers to the kidneys and the passageway between them to the Gold Pavilion.

LINE 43 The secrets of eternal birth are urgent in the Gold Pavilion.

LINE 44 The secular interpretation of the text, that immoral or lewd desire for sexual hygiene is meant here, is rejected.

LINE 45 The term *ts'un t'ien*, one-inch field, refers to the male yang principle, here interpreted to be the mixture of east's spring green and south's summer red within the Gold Pavilion, symbolized by a blue dragon and the trigram *ch'ien*. The term *ch'ih-t'a*, foot-high cottage, refers to the female yin principle, a

# The Gold Pavilion Classic; Taoist Emptying Meditation

combination of west's autumn white and north's winter darkness, mixed together in the Gold Pavilion to produce a white tiger and the trigram *k'un* (see page 121). The sexual hygiene school interprets the text to mean the joining of male and female organs. The spiritual or physical interpretation of the entire *Gold Pavilion* classic rests on these lines. The commentator chuckles at the non-Taoist use of this passage for physical purposes. To so misuse the text is to miss the core of Lao-tzu and Chuang-tzu's teaching on the Tao.

**LINE 46** By "forming the sphere," by remaining constantly aware of Tao's presence within the Gold Pavilion, the heart is at peace.

## Eighth Stanza (lines 47–52)

47 Watch the will, a wandering spirit, the three strange powers;
48 Only when emptied and void is the heart filled with peace.
49 Constantly focus on the Jade Pavilion, bright spirit will be present.
50 At all times retain the vast deep blue, never hunger or thirst.
51 Thus you will make the six *ting* (*yin*) ladies have audience there.
52 Close off intuition's outward path, eternal life is yours.

**LINE 47** When the will is activated, it becomes a wandering spirit, always looking outward to satisfy the heart's desires. The three sources of a wandering will are the "three worms," here called three *ling*, soul powers. The first worm resides in the head, destroying ch'i energy by judgments. The second worm resides in the heart, destroying the will with desires for fame, wealth, and glory. The third worm dwells in the belly, causing ching emotions and intuitive awareness to flow away after pleasure and sensations.

**Line 48** Only when the heart-mind "fasts," abstains from judgments and selfish desires, is the soul truly at peace.

**LINE 49** By awareness of Tao's presence in the Gold Pavilion, the whole body and all of its spiritual energies are enlightened, filled with a bright light. The term *shen-ming* can also mean "bright spirits," a term taken from folk religion referring to the spiritual forces of nature that bring blessing to humankind. But the commentary takes the term to mean that breath, spirit, and intuitive essence are thereby "made bright," enlightened by Tao's presence.

**LINE 50** The thirst and hunger of the soul for Tao presence is satisfied by meditating in timely fashion on the Great Void, here seen as a deep sky blue. The heart cavity is visualized to be filled with the deep blue-purple aura of primordial breath, cleansing it of all thoughts and desires. Thirst and hunger for outer things are quelled by color visualization and inner focus.

**LINE 51** The six *ting* ladies refers to the six lines of the trigram *k'un*, the symbol of purified yin. Tao inseminates primordial breath into nature at the winter solstice, when yin is purest. The six *ting* ladies enter the heart and the Gold Pavilion. The body is filled with the blue-purple vapors of primordial breath, thereby bringing about *ch'ang-sheng*, eternal birthing.

**LINE 52** By closing off access of intuitive awareness to the outer world and focusing on Tao's presence in the center of the microcosm, one touches the principle of eternal life. Note that

# The Gold Pavilion Classic; Taoist Emptying Meditation

the awareness of the center is nourished by focusing the mind's eye on the circulation of breath from the throat to the lungs, down the *jen* passage in the front of the body to the feet, upward along the *tu* passage behind the legs through the backbone to the top of the head, and back down to the tip of the nose. Impure, angry, and negative thoughts are expelled by breathing outward through the mouth, while pure air is breathed in and circulated again from the nose. One assists the imagination to observe this process by consciously following it with half-closed eyes. As the ch'i is visualized to come up the spine and over the top of the head, the eyes roll upward in the sockets and then down again, following the breath as it is expelled through the mouth. In similar fashion, the eyes follow the circulation of the blue-purple breath from the heart down to the kidneys and upward again in the lesser circle, from the lower stomach and backbone upward to the top of the rib cage.

### Ninth Stanza (lines 53 –56)

53 In the middle of the central room, when spirit does there dwell,
54 The heart is cleansed of itself, not touched by the impure.
55 Visualize the five upper organs (*wu-tsang*) in time with the seasons.
56 Perfect, control the six lower organs (*liu-fu*), clean as purest white.

**LINE 53** These four lines are spoken by the six *ting* lady spirits,[1] teaching how the heart and the bodily organs are purified by the *Gold Pavilion* classic meditations. The *cheng-shih* central or "true" room is the Gold Pavilion. The spirit of the heart, ruler of the body, is meant to dwell there.

# The Gold Pavilion

**LINE 54** When the heart spirit is purified, all things fall into place by themselves. No sullied things or impurities can stain the clean of heart.

**LINE 55** Meditate on each of the five organs in timely fashion, for example, the liver is filled with bright green vapor in spring in the annual cycle, or between dawn and 11:00 A.M. in the daily cycle of sun and moon. If following the daily movements of the Big Dipper in the heavens, the Taoist meditates on liver, green, wood, spring, and the first key of the Lydian scale when the tail of the dipper points to the eastern quadrant. This system is explained more fully in a later section of the text. The organs follow in order:

| liver | east | spring | green | mi | morning | 1st and 2nd lunar months |
| heart | south | summer | red | sol | afternoon | 4th and 5th lunar months |
| lungs | west | autumn | white | do | evening | 7th and 8th lunar months |
| kidneys | north | winter | purple-blue | re | night | 10 and 11th lunar months |
| spleen | center | | gold | la | noon-midnight | 3rd, 6th, 9th, and 12th lunar months |

**LINE 56** The six lower organs, the stomach, colon, large and small intestines, gallbladder, urinary bladder, and the triple conduits (food, drink, ch'i breath), are affected by emotional attachment. Joy, sorrow, happiness, sadness, and anger, are controlled here. By awareness of Tao in the Gold Pavilion, the emotions are kept pure. A bright white color is envisioned to fill the lower body, bright as the whitest snow.

*Tenth Stanza* (lines 57–64)

57  When in the void transcendent state Tao is present of itself.
58  When things are let to be of themselves, affairs are no bother.

## The Gold Pavilion Classic; Taoist Emptying Meditation

❋

59  Like *ch'ui-hung* [North Star] nonmoving, the body is at peace.
60  The void dwelling place of the transcendent is within the tent,
61  Alone, in this solitary vast expanse, the mouth is speechless.
62  Quiet, unsullied, no desires, the wanderer arrives in the garden;
63  Clear, calm, fragrant, chaste, Jade Ladies are present.
64  Perfect the *te* breath, light pervades, gateway to the Tao.

**LINE 57** The term *hsü* refers to the heart-mind, which must be kept pure and void of all images and desires. *Wu* is the Tao, which eternally spins forth the single thread of ch'i breath, as in the *Tao-te Ching*, chapter 6, which is never exhausted. The Tao is of itself, *tzu* "of itself," *jan*, "it is thus." When the heart-mind is void, the Tao's presence is made known *tzu-jan* of itself.

**LINE 58** *Wu* refers to the myriad creatures that are spun forth from the Tao, as in the *Tao-te Ching*, chapter 42 (Tao births the One, Two, Three, and the myriad creatures). These things too, when left alone to be as they are (*tzu* of themselves, *jan* as they are), cause no trouble.

**LINE 59** If we are like *ch'ui-hung*, the North Star, immobile in the northern heavens while the cosmos circles around it, then our whole self will be at peace.

**LINE 60** The void dwelling place of the Tao is like a great tent or pavilion, inside of which the soul rests. The allusion here is to *huntun* (Hundun, in the seventh chapter of the *Chuang-tzu*), inside of which the two children, yang and yin, love to play.

**LINE 61** Inside of this vast expanse, face-to-face with Tao's presence, the mouth can utter no words.

**LINE 62** When the mind is clear and unsullied, and the heart is without desires, then the soul is free to wander in this garden of primordial breath. The term *te* (as in *Tao-te Ching*) is a synonym for ch'i, *t'ai-chi, yü-wei chih tao* (immanent Tao), and *huntun* (primordial nondifferentiation).

**LINE 63** The term *yü-nü* or Jade Ladies refers to the six lines of the trigram *k'un*, the purest form of earth, yin. When the heart-mind is fragrant with quiet and purity, the six yin ladies, symbols of the *te* of line 62, are present in the Gold Pavilion, singing and dancing before the Tao.

**LINE 64** Perfect the state of *te* purity, the void center will be filled with a bright light, gateway to Tao's presence. To perfect this state, the mind's ch'i energy, the heart's desires, and the belly's intuitive powers must be alchemically refined in this bright light, a fire that blends the three into one, the primordial state of *huntun*, in preparation for oneness with Tao.

II

*First Stanza* (lines 1–5)
1  Nourish Tao [path], wander in darkness, dwell alone in the deep.
2  Nurture form and destiny, keep the transcendent void empty.
3  Pure and clean is Transcendent Act, mind cannot conceive it.
4  Feathered wings cover *wu* and ch'i, carefully kept detached,
5  Eternal gestation, always watch it, fly off to immortal realms.

**LINE 1** To practice the Tao one must wander or roam in the "dark night," the realm kept separate from worldly pursuit of fame, wealth, and glory, to concentrate on the void abyss within.

# The Gold Pavilion Classic; Taoist Emptying Meditation

**LINE 2** The way to nourish one's bodily strength and good fortune is to preserve a pure and empty heart-mind.

**LINE 3** The condition of *wu-wei*, the transcendent giving act proper to the Tao, is a state that is without thought or worry.

**LINE 4** Like a chicken hatching its eggs beneath warm feathers, one should always keep one's center free and separate from worldly concerns. The center of the Gold Pavilion, when filled with primordial breath, spirit-will, and intuition, contains within itself the three principles of cosmic gestation. The point to be emphasized here is that these powers are to be protected and preserved within the Gold Pavilion. In the terms of internal alchemy, the drop of primordial yang in the center of the water trigram *k'an*, and the drop of yin in the center of fire trigram *li*, symbols of heart's desires and intuition's focus, are to be kept in a truly protected mode within the Gold Pavilion of the microcosm.

**LINE 5** The person who contemplates Tao's eternal birthing or gestating of primordial breath within will "fly upward" to the realm of the immortals.

## Second Stanza (lines 6–12)

6  The five movements, even and uneven, have a common root;
7  The three fives, breaths united, are thereby joined to "One."
8  Whoever desires to be one with them, polestar, sun, and moon,
9  Embrace jade, clasp the pearl, peace in one's inner room.
10 If you can grasp this, myriad troubles cease.
11 You have them within yourself, hold on, never let go!
12 Then is attained "no death," when one enters the gold room.

**LINE 6** The five elements each have a yin (even) and yang

## The Gold Pavilion

(uneven) aspect in the meditations of inner alchemy. There are twice five (ten) symbolic numbers assigned to facilitate the meditation: 2, 4, 6, 8, and 10 are yin, while 1, 3, 5, 7, and 9 are yang. Each element has a color, season, tone, organ, and symbol, as well as two numbers, to use in the meditation.

| east | green | spring | mi | liver | dragon | 3, 8 |
| south | red | summer | sol | heart | phoenix | 2, 7 |
| center | gold | middle | la | spleen | cauldron | 5, 10 |
| west | white | autumn | do | lungs | tiger | 4, 9 |
| north | purple | winter | re | kidney | tortoise | 1, 6 |

The numbers 1 through 5 are called the "raw" series because they lead inward to the transcendent Tao. The numbers 6 through 10 are the "cooked," because they lead outward to the changing, ripening, and harvesting world of *te* nature.

**LINE 7** The "three fives" refer to the raw set of numbers from 1 through 5, that is, east is 3, south is 2, west is 4, north is 1, and center is 5. The meditator becomes one with the eternally gestating Tao by making these numbers into three fives: east's wood (3) joined to south's fire (2) makes the first five. Center's gold earth (5) is the second five. West's metal (4) joined to north's water (1) makes the third five.

The meditation is done by visualizing colors, musical tones, and "breath" from the five bodily organs to be joined in the Gold Pavilion. Thus east's green and south's red are joined in the Gold Pavilion, and produce the deep violet color of primordial breath. Earth's gold is brought into the Gold Pavilion and refined into primordial spirit, a bright gold. West's white

## The Gold Pavilion Classic; Taoist Emptying Meditation

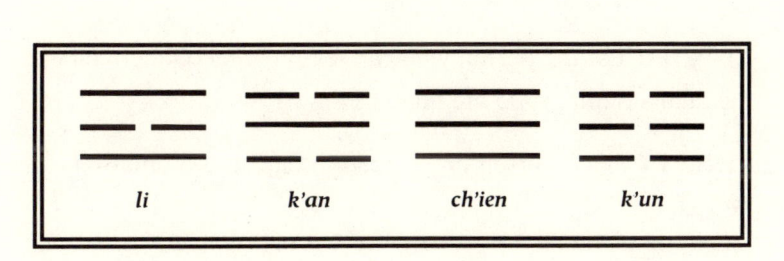

|  li  |  k'an  |  ch'ien  |  k'un  |

and north's dark blue are brought into the Gold Pavilion and refined by intuitive awareness of Tao's presence, a bright white. These "three fives" are joined as one with the Tao in meditation.

LINE 8 The person who would be one with this process, the very core and essence of the Gold Pavilion classic meditation, must also realize that the meditation includes contemplating the sun, the moon, and the polestar constellation Ursa Major.

LINE 9 To grasp the jade means to refine the drop of pure yin from within the "sun," the fire trigram *li*, which has a broken yin line in its center. To embrace the pearl means to pluck the drop of pure yang from the depths of the ocean, the unbroken yang line in the center of the water trigram *k'an*. Thus jade means pure yin; and the red fiery pearl, found atop most Chinese temples, symbolizes pure yang. The pearl is Tao-gestated primordial breath, in the depths of earth and ocean's yin. The seven stars of Ursa Major always point to the North Star, symbol of Tao as the cosmic center of nature. The six stars of the southern constellation (Scorpio) are symbols of the six Jade Ladies, pure yin in the cosmos. Thus north and south, sun and moon, *li* and *k'an* stand for the union of yin and yang within the Gold Pavilion, in the presence of the gestating Tao.

# The Gold Pavilion

**LINE 10** For the person who can learn the meditation, all of the affairs of the world are no longer a worry.

**LINE 11** Each person must grasp the method by himself or herself.

**LINE 12** The secret of immortality is simply to enter into the Gold Pavilion, aware of Tao's eternal presence.

*Third Stanza* (lines 13–17)

13 Go forth yang sun, enter yin moon, this is my Tao [path].
14 Heaven's seven, earth's three, return mutually preserved.
15 Ascend, descend, enter, exit, join together a long time.
16 The jade stone ornament is my precious treasure.
17 You have it within yourself, why not preserve it?

**LINE 13** The third stanza has three distinct interpretations of the spiritual, physical (sexual) hygiene and the breath exercise schools. The symbols of the five lines can be interpreted consistently in any of the three modes.

Sun is yang, the trigram *li*, fire, or male. Moon is yin, the trigram *k'an*, water, or female. The going forth *ch'u* or exit is through the heavenly gateway, the trigram *ch'ien*. The entrance *ju* is through the trigram *k'un* for earth.

**LINE 14** Heaven's seven and earth's three refer to the numbers of the prior heavens (*hsien-t'ien*), or *ho-t'u*, configuration of the *I Ching*. Seven is the number for fire. Three is the number for wood. Joined together they add up to ten, the central number of the *ho-t'u*, which symbolizes Tao as present. Fire or the trigram *li* is placed in the west in the *ho-t'u* chart, while wood

# The Gold Pavilion Classic; Taoist Emptying Meditation

and the trigram *k'an* are in the east. Thus when west's seven, fire, (conceived of as a white tiger, *li*) and east's three, wood (the trigram *k'an* seen as a blue dragon), are joined, the number ten, symbol of Tao's presence, is attained.

LINE 15 The interpretation of this passage is crucial for the three schools. The first interpretation can be explicitly sexual, if yin and yang are taken to mean the male and female organs. The sexual hygiene school teaches that male and female should unite in sexual activity for periods of long duration, without having orgasm or emission. Some modern American psychologists advocate use of this method in marriage counseling, which, though useful in bolstering the male self-image, misunderstands the goal of sexual hygiene. The practice was originally done to "preserve semen" (if a male), while stealing the female energies during intercourse. Reversed, the practice is used by a woman to steal male energies, while conserving her own. The practice was officially condemned by Confucian literati, Buddhist monks, and religious Taoist movements as chauvinist and without real or spiritual benefit.

The breath control or inner alchemy school interprets the text as circulation of breath and swallowing of saliva, as in the well-known schools of qigong, t'ai chi, and kung fu exercise.

The religious and monastic schools influenced by the great Taoist Lady Wei Huacun (d. fourth century C.E.) reject the sexual hygiene interpretation in favor of the "union with the Tao" as explained in this commentary. The colors of the five elements, combined from five into three, three into one, are circulated from the heart to the kidneys, in and out of the Gold

## The Gold Pavilion

❀

Pavilion, bringing awareness of the Tao's gestating presence within. The *ch'ien* or upward passage (the *tu* meridian in acupuncture) and the *yung* or downward passage (*jen* in acupuncture) are visualized as channels for breath and color circulation in and out of the Gold Pavilion. In ancient Chinese alchemy, what nature takes 5,096 days (2,048, 1,024, 512, 256, 128, 64, and so forth) to evolve, the meditator accomplishes in a single moment interiorly, refining "gold," centering awareness on Tao's gestating presence.

The elapsed time to be set aside for the awareness meditation is approximately forty minutes. The Chinese clock was divided into twelve *shih* hours, each shih being equivalent to two sixty-minute hours. Each hour was divided into six *hou* of twenty minutes each. The refining process of inner alchemy (*neitan*) requires two *hou*, or forty minutes. The meditation itself is divided into four stages, according to the *I Ching* mantic symbols, *yüan* (spring, planting, Tao breathing forth ch'i), *heng* (summer, ripening, hatching, sacrifice), *li* (autumn, harvest, storage), and *chen* (winter, rest, contemplation).

At the beginning of the time period the heart-mind directs its attention to *yüan*, the flow of primordial breath "between heaven and earth," between the purple cinnabar field in the head and the middle cinnabar field of the chest. Then the breath is *heng*, first heated by the red-robed spirit in the fires of the heart, then sent down to the somber spirits of the water in the two kidneys, to be given as an offering to the Gold Pavilion. Note that the five colors, green, red, gold, white, and deep blue, are *li* harvested from the five organs, refined in heart's fire (green plus red equals purple; gold equals gold; white and dark equal purified white), washed in kidney's

## The Gold Pavilion Classic; Taoist Emptying Meditation

❊

water, and mixed together into "one" for storage in the Gold Pavilion.

Finally the three colors purple, gold, and white, now dark and formless, are united with the Tao within the Gold Pavilion. They are charged to overflowing with the presence of the Tao gestating from the depths of the dark valley floor (*Tao-te Ching*, chapter 6). The intuition is held in the all-absorbing presence of the Tao for a prolonged time, protected by the six Jade Ladies, who represent the purest powers of gestating yin, freed from all desires for fame, profit, or sensual gratification (*Chuang-tzu*, chapter 1).

The person so meditating is said to be in the *hsien-t'ien*, the prior heavens, touching the transcendent gestating Tao (*wu-wei chih tao*). If the faintest suggestion of self-profit, self-glory, or self-gratification enters, then the meditation is tainted; the method reverts to that of the *hou-t'ien* posterior heavens, and no longer belongs to the Mao Shan Shang ch'ing (Highest Pure) or Chengi (True One) tradition of the Taoist Lady Wei Huacun.

LINE 16 The prior heavens are symbolized by the purest jade, on which are carved the figure of the *ho-t'u*, the precious *Ling-pao Chen-wen* describing the above forty-minute process of inner alchemy. The center of the *ho-t'u* has the number fifteen (five plus ten) inscribed on it, a sign of the Tao's eternally gestating presence. Once tasting this presence, the meditator no longer desires to return to worldly pursuits, the worries of fame, wealth, and desire, goals of the posterior heavens.

LINE 17 The Taoist does not distinguish between man and woman, rich and poor, intelligent and foolish. Every person has the ability to be aware of the Tao's presence within.

## The Gold Pavilion

*Fourth Stanza* (lines 18–21)

18  The heart that knows the root source nourishes a separate flower.
19  Serve heaven, follow earth, unite with ching in the storehouse.
20  Nine-Source Mountain stands alone [in the northern sea].
21  In its center lives a *chen-jen*, now you can command him.

**LINE 18** The meditator must harmonize yang and yin externally as well as internally. To do this is to know the source of strength in the Gold Pavilion. When the Gold Pavilion is filled to overflowing with Tao's primordial breath, then the eyes see only the bright, the ears hear only wisdom, the nose smells fragrance, the mouth tastes the sweet, the hair does not gray. This is the meaning of "nourish a separate flower"—awareness of Tao presence in the Gold Pavilion keeps all negatives away from external consciousness. The person filled with negative thoughts and feelings does not meditate on the Tao.

**LINE 19** To serve or swallow heaven means to join with the drop of green jade (yin) in the center of yang; that is, in the center of the sun is a drop of pure green jade, symbolizing purified intuition. To follow earth means to regulate and harmonize with the drop of pure yang in the depths of the ocean, the drop of primordial breath held between the kidneys, just below the Gold Pavilion. Ching intuition and ch'i primordial breath refined from the outer world are then joined by eidetic (extraordinarily clear and active) vision into Tao awareness, and stored or kept in the Gold Pavilion.

**LINE 20** Nine-Source Mountain is a mythical island in the northern sea, the home of primordial breath. Nine is a symbol

# The Gold Pavilion Classic; Taoist Emptying Meditation

❊

of yang or fire-purified breath. Here it refers to the spot between the kidneys, where breath is focused.

**LINE 21** On this island dwells the Tao-realized person of Chuang-tzu's fourth chapter, who sits in forgetfulness and fasts from all judgment or desire in the heart. The meditator has the ability to command this spirit; the mind controls the outward and inward flow of ch'i simply by being aware of the outer world and of Tao's gestating presence within.

*Fifth Stanza* (lines 22–27)

22  Interior yang, three spirits, can provide eternal birth.
23  For seven days with center's five, revolve, mutually joining.
24  Mount K'un-lun's peak, do not mistake or lose its location.
25  Hidden there is a purple palace with a cinnabar walled tower.
26  Boldly refine yang and yin into a bright red pearl,
27  For a myriad of years shining brightly, time itself stands still.

**LINE 22** Yang when interiorized has three spiritual functions. The first is *yüan-ch'i*, primordial breath's energy gestated from the Tao. The second is the spirit's power to know the outer world, to name, compare, and judge it. The third is the spirit focused on the Tao's presence in the Gold Pavilion, defined by Chuang-tzu as the *chen-jen*. These three spiritual functions are yang's powers. Primordial breath is used up by focusing on judgments and desires of the outer world. By focusing on Tao's inward presence, the yang powers are not used up. The meditator literally is one with Tao's constant birthing (*ch'ang-sheng*).

**LINE 23** For seven days practice circulating breath along the *jen* and the *tu* channels, keeping mind and therefore

# The Gold Pavilion

ch'i focused on Tao in the Gold Pavilion (centering meditation).

**LINE 24** Mount K'un-lun here refers to the point in between the kidneys, the entrance to the Gold Pavilion. The Gold Pavilion stands on the summit of Mount K'un-lun.

**LINE 25** Hidden to all but the meditator is the Gold Pavilion, atop Mount K'un-lun, surrounded by a deep glowing purple aura of primordial breath, within a walled tower made of cinnabar. Breath refined by meditatively joining east's (3) green wood with south's (2) red cinnabar fire produces primordial purple breath.

**LINE 26** Boldly take these two colors, the drop of green yin from the center of heart's *li* fire, and the drop of red yang from the center of ocean's *k'an* water, and refine the "bright red pearl" or the bright red cinnabar pill, symbol of ch'i breath, shen spirit, and ching intuition, fused in the alchemy of meditation.

**LINE 27** This hidden light is eternally bright, outside spatial and temporal changes.

*Sixth Stanza* (lines 28–31)
28 Root the self in outer yang, spirits of themselves will come;
29 Nourish the interior three yin, they too can eternally gestate.
30 The *hun* seeks ascent to heaven, *p'o* descends to the depths.
31 Reverse *hun*, exchange *p'o*, Tao and *tzu-jan* nature.

**LINE 28** Outer yang refers to the primordial Tao-gestated breath that comes from the earth, *k'un*. The outer world of nature in its pure yin state, the depths of the valley floor

## The Gold Pavilion Classic; Taoist Emptying Meditation

❋

(*Tao-te Ching*, chapter 6), is the true dwelling place of Tao. When the Taoist refines the three spirits (ch'i, shen, and ching), then the outer world as well is a source for realizing Tao presence, in the valley floor and the ocean depths, represented by the single yang line in the center of the trigram *k'an*. Such a person can nourish the three yang spirits from the exterior as well as the interior. The spirits of nature come to fulfill the summons.

**LINE 29** The three interior yang spirits, represented by the trigram *li*, each have a yin line in their center. The three yin spirits from the external world, represented by the trigram *k'an* each have a straight yang line in their center. Thus when the three yin spirits of the external world of nature join with the three yang spirits of the internal world of meditation, the three resulting trigrams are pure yang, the three unbroken lines of the trigram *ch'ien*. This is a symbol of the primordial breath eternally gestated by the Tao.

**LINE 30** In the normal course of life, the *hun* or yang parts of the human body leave at death; and after purification in the chemical fires of the underworld, they ascend to heaven. The seven *p'o* energies are buried with the body in the grave.

**LINE 31** In this meditation the yin and yang elements are fused together, so that the "seven" (symbol of the yin forces within) and the "nine" (three times three refined yang lines) are reversed. The yang energies are circulated downward through the *jen* channel into the purifying waters of the kidney. The yin energies are sent upward through the *tu* channel into the fires of the heart. Then all of the energies are poured together into the state of *huntun* (*Chuang-tzu*, chapter 7) in the center of the Gold Pavilion. Yang primordial breath is purple, yang spirit is gold, and purified ching

## The Gold Pavilion

intuition is white. The three colors, mixed in the Gold Pavilion, lose all color and are darkened (the state of *huntun*). It is at this point that Tao's gestating presence is realized.

### III

*First Stanza* (lines 1–11)

1. The Big Dipper, suspended pearls, bracelet without seam,
2. Jade *p'in*, gold flute, forever strong and firm,
3. Bear heaven, suspend earth, complete *ch'ien* and *k'un*.
4. The trigrams are four times red [ripe] as red can be,
5. Yang comes first, then *pi*, each in its opposite gate.
6. Accompany them, to refine the pill, enter the dark springs.
7. Fresh sprouts, turtle, lead breath to spirit source.
8. In the center is a Tao-realized person, cap made of gold.
9. Wearing armor, holding a talisman, he opens the seven gates.
10. Here no branch or leaves, indeed it is the root.
11. Day and night meditate on it, always aware of its presence.

**LINE 1** The entire stanza is filled with cryptic verse, requiring a master and an oral tradition to interpret meaningfully. The Big Dipper is seen as a string of suspended pearls in the northern heavens strung on a seamless thread. As it turns, it points eternally to pei-chi, the polestar, center of the heavens. It is a symbol of the meditator eternally aware of Tao's presence in the microcosmic center, the Gold Pavilion.

**LINE 2** The image now reverses the roles of yin and yang. Jade is symbol of the yin broken line in the center of the trigram *li*, a drop of pure yin in the center of fiery yang. Gold (metal) is the straight yang line in the center of the trigram *k'an*, a symbol

## The Gold Pavilion Classic; Taoist Emptying Meditation

of the drop of pure yang in the depths of the ocean. The Taoist meditator keeps these pure states of yang and yin firm by awareness of the internal process of Tao gestating ch'i, yang, and yin.

**LINE 3** Heaven's yang is compared to a necklace, and earth's yin to pearls strung thereon. The seven stars of the Big Dipper are pearls eternally revolving around the North Star, pointing to Tao in heaven's center. Thus seven (west, yin, metal, tiger, the drop of yang in the depths of yin) now becomes the male principle. In completing it's circling of the polestar every twenty-four hours, the Big Dipper always points to, or is focused on, Tao in the Gold Pavilion's center. The jade pool, the spot between the kidneys (water), which is the gateway to the Tao, is now the "male," the source of pure yang's union with the Tao.

**LINE 4** There are four appropriate times or seasons, in the meditation of inner alchemy, for conceiving and nourishing the "child within." The *ch'ih-tzu* ruddy child, also called the red cinnabar drop, is inseminated, nourished, matures, and rests in Tao awareness, just as the hexagrams cycle through *yüan, heng, li,* and *chen,* and the seasons pass through spring, summer, autumn, and winter. The four stages of Taoist meditation follow this process: *yüan* for inseminating breath, spirit, and intuitive awareness into the Gold Pavilion; *heng* for the three principles offering sacrifice to Tao in the center; *li* for harvesting the brightly glowing drop or "pearl," that is, pill, giving birth to the hierophant child within; and *chen* for dwelling quietly in the awareness of Tao's presence. This last stage takes place in the "tenth month" of the lunar year, the time for the communal celebration of the Taoist Chiao rites of renewal.

# The Gold Pavilion

❋

**LINE 5** The language here is derived from inner alchemy and acupuncture. The motion of the breath is *ni* contrary to the outward progression (Tao births One, Two, Three) of ch'i, yang, and yin to the myriad creatures of nature. The meditator works from the multiplicity of nature back to the origin, returning to the source in the wondrous Tao (Three, Two, One, to Tao).

**LINE 6** One sends the three principles back into the deep mysterious source within the Gold Pavilion. The deep dark springs (*hsüan-ch'uan*) is the north, the jade pool between the kidneys.

**LINE 7** The young green sprouts of spring, the "blue dragon," joined with south's fire, are refined into primordial breath and poured into "spirit root," Tao presence, from this place.

**LINE 8** The realized person in the center is primordial breath, refined into the hierophant child within. The gold cap symbolizes the number seven, the pure yang, the refined breath of lines 2 through 6.

**LINE 9** The hierophant is dressed in gold armor and carries a talisman in his right hand for opening the seven gates. These are the acupuncture points *t'ien-ken, weilü, hsia-chi, yü-chen, ming-t'ang, chung-lou, chiang-kung* (see page 149), through which breath is circulated in the process of alchemical refinement.

**LINE 10** These are not the branches and leaves of the outer body but access points to the spirit root in the Gold Pavilion.

**LINE 11** By focusing on this process night and day, the Taoist meditator becomes constantly aware of Tao's gestating presence.

# The Gold Pavilion Classic; Taoist Emptying Meditation

### Second Stanza (lines 12–16)

12 The immortal, the Taoist, do they not have shen spirit?
13 [They] cause ching to be preserved year by year.
14 Mortals all eat grain, taste the five flavors;
15 Only ingest great harmony, yin-yang ch'i.
16 Then, able to avoid death, be one with the heavens.

**LINE 12** The meditator is reminded again to be one with the *hsien-t'ien*, the Tao of the *ho-t'u* or prior heavens. In this configuration the Tao present in the center vivifies shen spirit.

**LINE 13** The Taoist also "preserves ching," keeps the emotions and intuition free from outer dissolution. The focusing of attention on Tao working inwardly and in outer nature is a day-by-day, month-by-month, and year-by-year endeavor.

**LINE 14** Ordinary people all nourish themselves with the five grains, savoring worldly flavors.

**LINE 15** Taoists nourish themselves on interior peace and harmony, the ch'i primordial breath of yin and yang.

**LINE 16** This is why they are able to evade death, by being one with the prior heavens.

### Third Stanza (lines 17–25)

17 To know how to explain the five organs, each with a direction,
18 Realize that the heart spirit is king, ruler of the five organs.
19 When thoughts in the center move and rest, ch'i power leaves.
20 When the Tao of its own holds us, shen spirit is a bright light,
21 Throughout the day shining radiant, at night preserved within us.
22 When parched it quenches our thirst, hungry it makes us full.

*The Gold Pavilion*

23  Pass through the six *fu*, store there yang and yin.
24  Refine yang's drop of yin, save it in nine [heaven's gate].
25  Those who continually practice this will not know old age.

**LINE 17** Each of the five organs has a direction, color, season, number, and symbol. The Taoist must know how to explain this to do the meditation. (See line 55 of chapter I, page 115).

**LINE 18** The meditator must also know that the spirit of the heart is king of the entire body; the power of will controls the preserving or losing of mind's ch'i energy.

**LINE 19** When the thoughts in our mind control our movement and rest, then ch'i flows away.

**LINE 20** If the Tao in the Gold Pavilion holds my attention, then the soul-spirit will be filled with a bright light.

**LINE 21** It shines forth all day, nourishes inwardly at night. Shen is yang, bright, fire, heart, the trigram *li*, while ching is yin, dark, water, kidneys, and the trigram *k'an*.

**LINE 22** When thirsty, Tao quenches our thirst, when hungry our stomach is filled.

**LINE 23** The awareness fills our six lower organs as well, storing yang and yin energies there.

**LINE 24** Refine the drop of yang in the center of yin, and with it stand before the Tao in the prior heavens.

**LINE 25** The person who practices this peaceful awareness will not grow weak in old age.

## The Gold Pavilion Classic; Taoist Emptying Meditation

✻

### Fourth Stanza (lines 26–49)

26 The liver is the place whence ch'i is continuously refined,
27 Passing through the five organs, it generates three lights.
28 Above it harmonizes the *san-chiao*, refreshing all below.
29 Ching ministers heaven and earth's gates, eternal birth's Tao.
30 My shen spirit, *hun* and *p'o* both, are in the Gold Pavilion.
31 Ching flows to the inner source, fragrance reaches the nose.
32 Stand in the depths of the chest, within the *ming-t'ang*.
33 Penetrate to the *hua-ch'ih*, regulate yin and yang.
34 Then return to the mystery gate, serve heaven's Tao.
35 The approach is within my body, I who must preserve it.
36 Pure, be still, transcend action, will's motion will cease.
37 Ching and ch'i move up and down, regulating each passageway.
38 The seven openings, one with center, know not old age.
39 Returning, they sit at heaven's gateway, to serve yin and yang.
40 Descend through the throat, one with enlightened spirit,
41 Pass beneath the *hua-kai* canopy, pure and refreshed.
42 Plunge into the pure clear water, see my true form.
43 When time is ripe, pill is formed, eternal birth enabled.
44 Again pass through the *hua-ch'ih*, move the kidneys' ching.
45 Look up to the *ming-t'ang*, approach the cinnabar field.
46 Now let all the spirits open *mingmen*, life's gate.
47 Arrived, harvest heaven's Tao, stored at spirit root.
48 Yin and yang's broad expanse, as the endless flow of stars.
49 Liver's ch'i breath is like a bracelet, perfect without seam.

**LINE 26** The liver is the place where breath is meditatively refined.

*The Gold Pavilion*

❁

**LINE 27** It flows through the body's organs, giving birth to three lights, one each from sun, moon, and stars.

**LINE 28** It joins to the *san-chiao*, the "triple warmer" acupuncture points in the upper body, where it is heated by the spiritual fire, of line 27, the ripening "summer" part of the meditation. Then it flows downward to provide "refreshing drink" to the other bodily organs, "irrigating" the new life within.

**LINE 29** The ching intuitive awareness also is made to be aware of (minister to) heaven and earth's Tao of eternal birth.

**LINE 30** My soul-spirit, with its *hun* or yang aspects (liver, wood, spring, green) and its *p'o* or yin aspects (lungs, metal, autumn, white), is now focused on and led into the Gold Pavilion.

**LINE 31** When the ching intuitive awareness has flowed into the Gold Pavilion (Tao's presence), a fragrance arises and is perceived by the nose. The nose breathes in and out the pure ch'i gestated by the Tao. Note that spiritual fragrance (or lack of it) is detectable by proximity to the meditator.

**LINE 32** Attention is now focused on the *ming-t'ang*, the bright palace in the center of the chest, abode of spirit.

**LINE 33** Here the heart-spirit regulates the flow of air in (yang) through the nose, and out (yin) through the mouth, in the beginning stages of meditation. Then it regulates the flow of ch'i purified breath from the heart to the kidneys, in the advanced stage of meditation. The term *hua-ch'ih*, flowery pool,

## The Gold Pavilion Classic; Taoist Emptying Meditation

refers to the mouth in the first stage of meditation, and to the kidneys in the second.

**LINE 34** The soul-spirit then returns to the mystery gate, where it too "waits on" and is subservient to Tao.

**LINE 35** The approach to the Tao's eternally gestating presence takes place in the cosmic center of the body. Awareness, preserved there, brings about autumn's "harvest" of the immortal pearl.

**LINE 36** When the mind is quelled and purified of all judgment, then the heart rests in awareness of the *wu-wei* transcendent Tao and no longer runs after external fame, power, or wealth.

**LINE 37** The ching intuitive awareness and the ch'i purified breath are refined into one essence; intellect is quelled and intuition alone is active. This quiet alpha state passes through all the organs of the body, bringing peace and health.

**LINE 38** The seven apertures, the eyes, ears, nostrils, and mouth, described in the *Chuang-tzu*, chapter 7, bring about the death of *huntun*, inner awareness of Tao, when opened. Now when focused on Tao in the center, the body no longer feels the aging process.

**LINE 39** The five senses (seven apertures, that is, two eyes, two nostrils, two ears, one mouth) also sit at the gateway to the Gold Pavilion, watching yin-yang's gestation.

**LINE 40** When the breath first passes down through the throat into the lungs, it is first purified in the bright fires of the

## The Gold Pavilion

heart, and in this process it makes spirit bright, enlightened. Focusing attention on breathing, the cessation of judging others, enlightens the soul.

**LINE 41** The breath is circulated within the canopy of the chest, under the *hua-kai*, the upper rib cage, above the lungs and chest, down to the purifying and cooling waters of the kidneys.

**LINE 42** When one looks at oneself from the lower cinnabar field, the centering place between the kidneys, at the entrance to the Gold Pavilion, then one's real self is truly seen.

**LINE 43** The timely practice of the meditation, the planting, watering, growing, harvesting (the refined cinnabar pearl), and meditating quietly on Tao presence, is analogous to the cycling of the seasons. If one practices this, then like the seasons and the annual rebirth of nature at the solstice, one can attain to union with the eternal process of Tao gestating in nature.

**LINE 44** One must repeatedly pass through the "flower pool" (kidneys), moving ching intuition.

**LINE 45** Then with the will from above in the *ming-t'ang* bright palace of the heart, approach the lower cinnabar field.

**LINE 46** Then bring all of the spirits together to open the gateway to the Tao (this refers to the Inner Chapters of the *Gold Pavilion* classic).

**LINE 47** Now one can harvest (autumn) heaven's Tao and store it in spirit's root (Gold Pavilion).

**LINE 48** Tao gives birth to ch'i, yin, and yang, spreading them everywhere, even to the farthest stars.

## The Gold Pavilion Classic; Taoist Emptying Meditation

**LINE 49** The bright green ch'i breath from the liver, when purified in the above manner, is compared to a jade bracelet that is eternally circulating through the body, so perfectly formed that no seam or flaw appears on its surface.

### Fifth Stanza (lines 50–67)

50 The lungs process ch'i after passing through the *san-chiao*;
51 Returning to heaven's gate, it serves the ancient Tao.
52 Pure [ching] waters from lower source penetrate the six *fu*,
53 Flowing from the nose up and down, awakening the ears.
54 Contemplate heaven and earth, aware of the child within.
55 Regulate, harmonize ching flower, hair and teeth renewed.
56 Facial color bright and fresh, aged yet not turned white.
57 Passing it down from throat, how can it be scattered?
58 Let all the spirits come together, mutually seek the pure.
59 Proceeding down into the heart, petals of purple color
60 Stored hidden in the *hua-kai*, fall on all the organs,
61 Swirling, gather all the spirits, spread by *hu* breath.
62 Now see all of my inner spirits reject the lewd and vulgar.
63 The spleen spirit returns, relying on this great family.
64 It too is stored in spirit root, never again withered.
65 Then at last stomach region is one with void transcendent.
66 Lock and bolt the *mingmen* [life's gate], elegant like jade.
67 Longevity for a million years, and then some to spare.

**LINE 50** The function of the lungs in the meditation of internal alchemy is explained in these verses. The lungs process breath by passing ch'i through the triple warmers, the *san-chiao*, which here refer to the acupuncture points through which energy is circulated upward from the base of the lungs through the entire body.

LINE 51 Once ch'i has been breathed in through the nostrils and seen to pass through the entire body, the mind focuses on the *t'ien-men*, the gate of heaven, which here stands for the entrance to the Gold Pavilion where ch'i now comes to rest. The commentary says that the primordial breath of the lungs (the west, metal refined into liquid-water) is in fact ching intuition; mind is no longer focused on word, judgment, and meaning but rather has become an agent for intuitive awareness of Tao's presence, by being focused on *t'ien-men*.

LINE 52 The purified breath that has entered heaven's gate is now circulated through the six lower organs of the body, the large and small intestines, pancreas, *san-chiao*, gallbladder, and stomach, symbolically purifying the six emotional powers (joy, sorrow, anger, delight, aversion, attraction).

LINE 53 The air circulates in through the nose, down and up again through the body, and is expelled. This process makes the body extremely sensitive to the Tao's gestating process, both internal and external. The meditator hears sounds from great distances; birds, children, wild and domestic animals from the valley below echo in the sensitive ears on the mountaintop.

LINE 54 The joining of the west's two lungs (the trigram *ch'ien*, metal, white tiger) and the east's liver (the trigram *k'un*, wood, blue dragon) creates primordial ch'i breath. The joining of the north's two kidneys (the trigram *k'an*, water, tortoise) and

# The Gold Pavilion Classic; Taoist Emptying Meditation

the south's heart (the trigram *li*, fire, phoenix) creates purified ching intuitive essence. When primordial ch'i breath and refined ching are brought together in the Gold Pavilion, then the new child within is born, the ruddy hierophant.

**LINE 55** Doing the meditation keeps the meditator young.

**LINE 56** Light radiates from the face, the hair is not gray.

**LINE 57** Breathe in and down the throat, then where to focus attention?

**LINE 58** Where the spirits congregate, at the Gold Pavilion gate.

**LINE 59** Coming down through the red palace of the heart, the ch'i takes on a purple flower hue.

**LINE 60** Cached from *hua-kai* (ribs) to *liu-fu* (six lower organs) depths, the purified ch'i breath and ching intuition nourish the entire body on their journey to the Gold Pavilion.

**LINE 61** All of the "spirits," the spiritual powers of the body (the Taoist's *lu* list of spirits gives each a name), are purified and refined by breathing this Tao-gestated breath.

**LINE 62** As spirit is purified, all sensuous, impure, and selfish thoughts are washed away and henceforth avoided.

**LINE 63** The spleen is the organ wherein the healing gold color of purified earth spirit is stored during meditation. Just as heart and kidneys produce purified ching, and lungs with liver refine primordial ch'i breath, now all of the spirits of the body are purged of any negative elements and refined into bright gold

# The Gold Pavilion

shen in the spleen. Note that the five colors have now become three: purple ch'i, gold shen, and white ching.

**LINE 64** Store these three colors, purple, gold, and white, in the Gold Pavilion, they will never fade or wither. Note that when the three pure colors fade, they become the three worms, the *san-ch'ung* that devour the mind, heart, and belly. Ch'i becomes dull blue from sad thoughts; shen becomes dull yellow by negative judgments; and ching becomes a deathly gray-white by dwelling on impure or lewd thoughts. Spiritual death follows.

**LINE 65** The stomach passage here is the Gold Pavilion, the entrance to the Gold Pavilion. When the three pure colors are poured into this central place, the meditator is one with the void transcendent. The commentary here mentions the "five grains" (*wu-ku*) that must be avoided for effective internal alchemy. Besides heavy white starches, meats, eggs, fish, and strong spices are also shunned by the practitioner for physical as well as spiritual health.

**LINE 66** There is only an entrance, not an exit, to the Gold Pavilion, if the meditator maintains awareness of Tao's presence. The term *mingmen* (lifegate) here refers to the acupuncture point halfway up the spine that marks the top of the Gold Pavilion, the upper extent of the path of ch'i and ching as they circulate between the heart and kidney region, prior to entrance into the Gold Pavilion. The meditator forms an image of the heart's red fires creating the child within, the cinnabar pearl in the body's center.

**LINE 67** The person who does this meditation is not tired by

# The Gold Pavilion Classic; Taoist Emptying Meditation

the process even for a million years, and then some to spare. The process of refining breath and purifying spirit is done thus.

## Sixth Stanza (lines 68–78)

68 The spirit of the spleen travels to the center palace [heart];
69 In audience it regulates the five shen, forms three lights.
70 Above it joins with heaven's breath, one with the *ming-t'ang*.
71 It penetrates the six lower organs, tunes the five movers.
72 Metal, wood, water, fire, earth, master of each one.
73 It travels through the blood vessels, one with body's sweat.
74 The three spirits each attain it, and descend into Jade Flower.
75 Above, meet with primordial breath, years of life extended.
76 Carefully guard the seven outlets, keep out ill-fated events.
77 Sun and moon [light] spread everywhere, strengthen yin and yang.
78 Nourished by the Great Yin, become their true form.

**LINE 68** In the oral teachings of the Mao Shan tradition, attributed to the Lady Wei Huacun, when the above meditation is performed, the meditative chart known as *ho-t'u* is symbolically planted in the body. In this state the meditations of line 6 in chapter II, and the configuration of the five elements is reversed. Fire in the south moves to the west, and metal in the west moves to the south. Thus, east's wood (liver) is now burned by west's fire. The breath in the bellows of the lungs purifies the mind and produces primordial breath.

In similar manner, the metal of south (now in the central red palace of the heart) is refined by the waters of the north located in the kidneys; the result of the fires of inner alchemy is

*The Gold Pavilion*

purified ching, the intuitive awareness of Tao present in the Gold Pavilion. The central organ of the peritoneal region, the spleen, with its bright purified gold color, now takes over the role of *chu-shen*, the master spirit of the five organs. It travels into the heart palace, the place from which the entire body is governed by will.

**LINE 69** The five elements now come to have audience in the heart and are regulated by the healing gold light of the spleen spirit. It diffuses its healing rays through the body, joining to the three sources of "light," the purple, gold, and white aura of lines 59-64.

**LINE 70** It passes through and purifies the upper parts of the body, the breath of heaven in the head (pineal gland) and the *ming-t'ang* heart. These are the upper and middle cinnabar fields (*shang tan-t'ien, chung tan-t'ien*) in Taoist meditative terminology.

**LINE 71** It then flows down to the lower parts of the body and purifies the six lower organs, regulating the work of the five moving elements there. Note that the so-called five elemental movers, wood-spring, fire-summer, metal-autumn, water-winter, and earth-center, are temporal as well as spatial regulators. Thus the meditator determines the color, organ, and direction from which to initiate the meditation according to the hour, day, month, and year, as explained in the Inner Chapters of the *Gold Pavilion* classic.

**LINE 72** The spleen spirit has now become the master of metal, wood, water, fire, and earth.

**LINE 73** The gold healing light fills all of the blood vessels,

## The Gold Pavilion Classic; Taoist Emptying Meditation

the sweat glands, every pore of the body. The oral tradition insists at this point that "gold" is the symbol of the mind freed from negative judgments, and eventually from any judgments; verb is not joined to noun in the mind that contemplates in the transcendent Tao presence.

**LINE 74** Only when the three spirits, the purified form of ch'i, shen, and ching, are filled with this purifying light (mind emptied of judgment, will of desire for external wealth, intuition from emotional attachment, as in the *Chuang-tzu*, chapter 4), can they proceed into the presence of the Tao in the Gold Pavilion.

**LINE 75** Looking upward at the Tao, as one enters the Gold Pavilion, the vision of *yüan-ch'i* Tao-gestated life breath, described in chapter 6 of the *Tao-te Ching*, is seen. This vision is such that the meditator desires to remain within the state of contemplation, undisturbed by the passing of the years. The word for year, *nien*, bears the connotation of harvest, here meaning that years are extended by being eternally one with the Tao's gestating process.

**LINE 76** This line is an allusion to the *Chuang-tzu*, chapter 7, the story of Huntun (*huntun*). Yin and Yang drill seven holes in Huntun, two eyes, two ears, two nostrils, and a mouth. Thereupon Huntun, a symbol of the person focused on Tao presence, dies. To keep *huntun*, the meditation on the Tao, alive, the seven apertures must be closed to external glory, fame, wealth, and sensual gratification. The allowing of any worldly or selfish motives into the heart-mind is *pu-hsiang*, a harbinger of misfortune.

**LINE 77** The cycling process of sun and moon is the cause of seasonal, monthly, and daily changes in the cosmos. When united with the primordial condition of yin and yang, continually gestated from Tao, they become instead a source of eternal birth. Note that the term *ch'ang-sheng* does not mean eternal life but rather eternal birthing, in this context. Tao gives birth to One (primordial breath), an eternally gestating process.

**LINE 78** The Great Yin (*t'ai-yin*) is the eternally gestated ch'i breath, the drop of yang or bright flaming red pearl in the depths of the ocean. This symbol appears on most temple rooftops, with two rampant dragons shown devouring the flaming pearl. The dragon is the mythical animal who by devouring the Tao-gestated breath from the depths of the ocean, springs into the sky and causes the rains of spring, the source of new life and growth in nature. The Great Yin in the depths of the ocean thus achieves its true form, bringing new life within the meditating Taoist.

### Seventh Stanza (lines 79–99)

79 Of the five organs, the kidneys are the master of ching.
80 Go forth and come in these two gates, unite in the Gold Pavilion.
81 Inhale, exhale in the void transcendent, see my true form.
82 Strengthen the sinews and bones, perfect the blood vessels.
83 Dim and hidden, unseen, pass through pure spirit.
84 Sit beneath the grass hut, contemplate the little child.
85 Morning and evening be in the presence of spirit's bright light.
86 Exit by the nonbeing gate, enter by the transcendent door.
87 Purified, without selfish desires, nurture pure spirit.

## The Gold Pavilion Classic; Taoist Emptying Meditation

88 Nourished by ingesting purple breath, reach birth's source.
89 Return, again close the seven gates, drink from *t'ai-hsüan*.
90 Let it too go down the throat, pass through spirit root.
91 Ask about the immortal Tao, and its wondrous ways?
92 The answer is: ingest spirit mushroom, Jade Flower,
93 Wear a plain white cap on the head, feet in the cinnabar field.
94 Bathe in a flower-filled pool, water the spirit root.
95 Let all three channels attain it [breath], open *mingmen*.
96 Instead of the five flavors, exchange them for shan good breath.
97 The Great Tao is broad and vast, let heart be no longer worried.
98 Let down your hair over your shoulder, be always in Tao presence.
99 Now my Tao-way is completed, don't wrongly pass it on.

**LINE 79** The last stanza teaches how to circulate intuitive ching awareness, purified in the kidneys, through the body.

**LINE 80** Recalling the opening stanzas of chapter I, the kidneys are two gateways, entrance and exit, to the Gold Pavilion.

**LINE 81** By breathing or circulating breath within the center of the body, one becomes aware of the Tao child within. The basic goal of the *Gold Pavilion* classic is to remain focused on this centering spot in the body, aware of Tao's gestating presence.

**LINE 82** By so doing, by eliminating negative thoughts and selfish desires, the body becomes strong.

**LINE 83** One cannot see this process until actually focusing one's awareness on the spot between the kidneys, after purifying the spirit by the meditations of internal alchemy.

LINE 84 One sits in the eidetic (vivid, moving image) meditation before the Gold Pavilion, here described as a grass hut, and contemplates the child within. The ruddy infant, the real self, is playing in the presence of the gestating Tao.

Line 85 The adept is aware, day and night, of this presence.

LINE 86 The "no gate" or "transcendent door" leads to the Tao.

LINE 87 "Without selfish desires" means ending the search for glory, fame, and wealth and nourishing instead the spirit root within.

LINE 88 Spiritual nourishment is here symbolized by the circulation of the purple aura of primordial breath through the body. *Hsüan-ch'i* refers in Taoist terminology to the work of the Tao in the cosmos as gestating. Thus the meditator is told to be aware of the Tao's eternal act of gestating primordial breath, like a thread eternally spun from the depths within one's own body. The reference again is to the *Tao-te Ching*, chapter 6.

LINE 89 The meditator closes the seven apertures, as in line 76, a quote from the *Chuang-tzu*, chapter 7. The term *t'ai-hsüan* (*t'ai-yüan*) Great Abyss refers to the kidneys. To drink from the Great Abyss means specifically to be nourished by Tao's presence.

LINE 90 The passing of breath and saliva down the throat into the lower body, and the visualization of breath circulating between the heart and kidneys, is summarized here.

LINE 91 The author now reviews the *Gold Pavilion* teachings.

# The Gold Pavilion Classic; Taoist Emptying Meditation

**LINE 92** The Jade Mushroom is the drop of pure yang ch'i that is born from the depths of yin, the trigram *k'an* or water. The Jade Flower is the drop of pure yin ching intuitive awareness

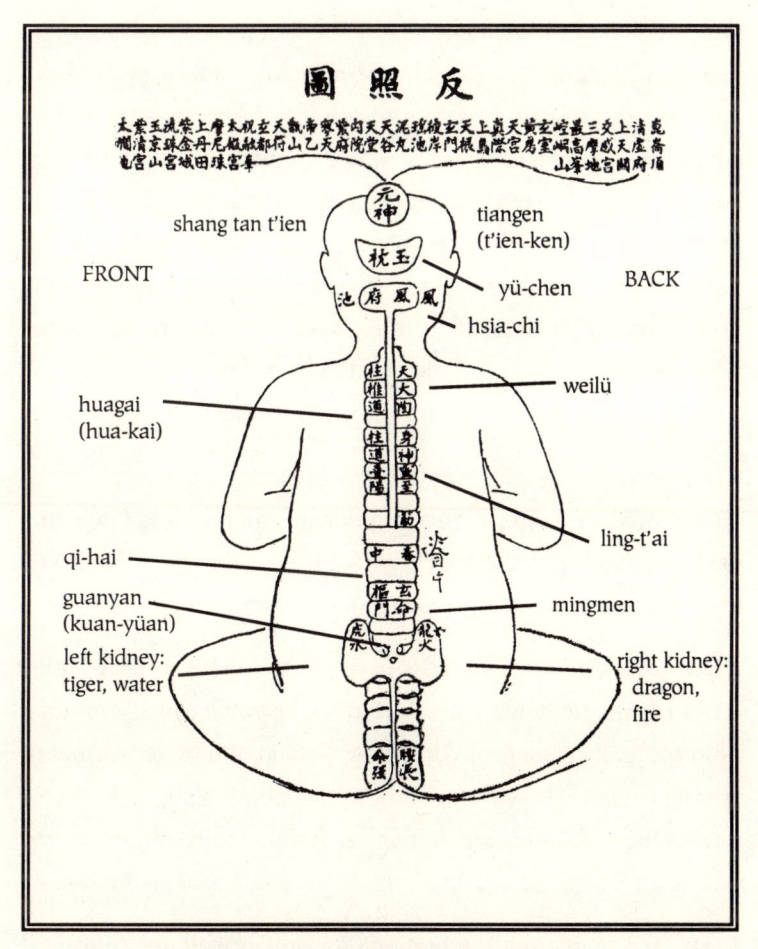

*Meditation and acupuncture points,
Ch'ing dynasty woodblock print from* Xingming Guizhi.

# The Gold Pavilion

born in the depths of yang, the trigram *li* or fire. Spirit, when nourished by or joined with these two purified energies, can enter the Gold Pavilion.

**LINE 93** The white cap worn by the Taoist is here a symbol of the west and the element metal. The liturgical cap of the Mao Shan and Chengi Taoist is made of gold metal, a symbol of meditatively purified breath and intuition. Into the top of the gold crown is placed a small flame-shaped pin, symbolizing that the Taoist is alive with the flames of alchemical meditation and has formed the ruddy child within. "Feet in the cinnabar field" refers to the *yü-pu* dance of *yü*, whereby the body as well as the internal awareness of the Taoist is moved to audience with the Tao. Thus the Taoist meditates in private and dances in public ritual to the presence of the gestating Tao.

**LINE 94** The pool filled with flowers is the kidneys and the space between, from which one meditates on the Gold Pavilion. Once purified, the "waters," the intuition, flow into the Gold Pavilion to irrigate spirit root, Tao's presence.

**LINE 95** The term *san-fu* can mean the twice three, or six, lower organs (in some commentaries), or in the Mao Shan tradition it refers specifically to the *san-chiao*, the triple warmers, spiritual channels within the body for conducting ch'i, shen, and ching into the Gold Pavilion. Acupuncture charts show points for accessing the *san-chiao* for healing and meditation.

**LINE 96** Once the meditations are under way, the body no longer feels the need to be nurtured by the five flavors, but instead nourishes others by *shan* good deeds of healing, and by positive feelings toward all others.

## The Gold Pavilion Classic; Taoist Emptying Meditation

**LINE 97** Awareness through meditation of the Tao's gestating presence leads to a calmness of heart and a lack of worry about past or future events. Worries from the past or future are only in the mind. Awareness of the present heals strain, stress, and illness occurring from negativity. Tao's presence is positive.

**LINE 98** The traditional Taoist, both man and woman, let the hair grow long, lived and ate simply, observed celibacy (unless married and dwelling in the city), and meditated in the above fashion. The married Taoist passed on the meditative and ritual teachings to a son or daughter, and the celibate mountain-dwelling Taoist passed on the *Gold Pavilion* classic meditative tradition and its ritual dramatic expression to chosen disciples.

**LINE 99** With these lines, the Outer Chapters of the *Gold Pavilion* classic come to an end. The reader is warned to pass on these teachings in the correct, pure form, rather than in the heterodox or lewd commercial manner of sexual hygiene or the harmful, self-aggrandizing martial arts. The tradition of Taoist meditation and ritual, and the philosophy of Lao-tzu and Chuang-tzu, are united in this Mao Shan Highest Pure Taoist tradition.

## ❊ Chapter Five

# Tantric Meditation

The introduction to Taoist meditation given in chapters 1 and 2 acquaints the reader with a nonjudgmental way of thinking that brings great interior peace and tranquillity. The symbols and imagery of chapter 4 can only be understood after learning to focus attention on the body's center and to envision the bright healing colors of nature, taught in chapter 3. The imagination, once awakened by this visualization process, begins to develop new creative powers and takes quiet pleasure in contemplation. The newly acquired ability to create sacred images utilizes the entire person. The body dances, the heart sings, and the mind contemplates in the presence of the transcendent or the sacred. This form of total body prayer is called Tantric meditation.

The use of body, mouth, and mind in harmony during prayer is found in all religious traditions. The *Spiritual Exercises* of Saint Ignatius of Loyola, the simplified chant and dance of the Islamic Sufi tradition, and the Tantric Buddhism of Tibet (and to some extent of Japan) all use the entire body as a single unit when praying.[1] The word *Tantric* describes the Buddhist version of total immersion in prayer. The use of mudra hand dance, mantra chant, and mandala (cosmically centered, geometrically patterned) meditation means in practice that body, mouth, and mind work in intricate harmony during prayer, leading to the emptying of mental images and selfish desires before transcendent union.

There are two other physical ways of prayer leading to emptiness in the Asian tradition. The first is the concentration of mind attained when sitting, as in Zen (Chan, dhyana) or centering (Samatha-vipasyana) meditation. The second is the devotional chanting of sutras or phrases. Various Pure Land Buddhist schools follow the method of devotional chant.[2] These two forms of practice have become more popular in the West than Tantric prayer during the twentieth century, and are the subject of a lively Buddhist-Christian dialogue. Though many Western church officials, both Protestant and Catholic, look on Buddhist and other non-Christian forms of prayer with some suspicion, in fact the Zen and Tantric methods themselves have no doctrinal content and can be practiced without changing the belief, visual images, or faith of the practitioner.

There are two very real obstacles to practicing the meditations of kenosis or emptying both in Asia and in the West. The first is the busy life of the monk or professional clergy, which leaves little time apart from monastic chant or rectory (temple) management to teach the prayer of "emptiness" to the laity. The temple chant, pious discourse, and the Sunday sermon focus on morality, human needs, and scriptural exegesis rather than on methods of contemplation. Laity are provided limited access to contemplative prayer, though they may seek far more than the Sunday sermon anecdotes and piety.

A second obstacle is found in the personal life of the priest, nun, monk, or clergyman. A life that started out as a spiritual quest becomes that of an overworked functionary who counsels the suffering, offers prayers for the needs of the faithful, heals the sick, and buries the dead. The Sunday service with sermon in the West and the public chanting of Buddhist sutras in Asia cease to be oriented toward the prayer of union that defines the mystic experience and instead become involved in the offering of prayers asking for things, or sermons on morality extolling virtue and condemning vice. Such prayers fill the mind of the laity with nonsacred images. Religion loses all meaning and function other than as a petitionary or moralizing service for specific material needs. The mass exodus from religious services in the West and the sole use of Buddhist chant for "merit" in Asia are the direct results of these kataphatic or image-filling devices. The Sunday sermon that promotes virtue and berates evil causes that which is evil to be visualized and kept in memory. Good and bad images, such as crime portrayed on a television screen, desired consumer goods such as expensive cars, clothing styles, and accumulated wealth are visualized in prayer and ritual.[3]

The Tantric way of kenosis or mystic prayer, on the other hand, removes all but sacred images from the memory screen. The mind is no longer involved in worries about health and illness, praise and blame, success or failure, but is instead taken up with the awareness of sacred presence. In this condition, any thought, good or bad, is seen as a distraction from the state of transcendent awareness. The way of kenosis or emptying prayer ceases to be the monopoly of the priestly or religious caste. Any person, laity or monk, businessperson or nomad, may practice it.

Learning the way of kenosis or emptying prayer involves three phases. These three stages are recognized in Western theology and African and Asian contemplative sources. The stages are as follows:

- Purgation or purification
- Illumination or visualization of the sacred
- The emptying of all images, or the "Dark night," which precedes mystic union or awareness of the absolute.[4]

Having successfully completed the three phases of emptying prayer, the meditator experiences transcendent union or awareness. The authenticity of the mystic experience is verified by a subsequent life of selfless compassion.

The way of purgation or purification is always the first step toward true contemplative prayer. It is not the same as the "dark night" or emptying process called kenosis that empties the mind of sacred images. Rather, it is the prelude to all forms of prayer and creative visualization. The person involved in negative judgment, physical need (whether hunger or ill health), drugs or alcohol of any form, and selfish pursuit that harms or puts down others must first be purified and made whole before proceeding to the second and third stages of contemplative prayer. All Asian forms of prayer experience, including the Buddhist, Taoist, Altaic shaman, and pan-Asian medium, begin with strict rites of purification. Fire and water are both physical and symbolic images used in this process.[5]

## Tantric Meditation

The shortcomings of the Christian Sunday sermon system are to be found here. The laity are continually exposed to verbal descriptions of good and bad behavior but are rarely led beyond purgative images to a life of contemplative visualization (contemplating the life of Jesus, for example, in the Christian context, as explained in Ignatius's *Spiritual Exercises*). Western clerics could lead the laity into higher forms of contemplative prayer, because they themselves practice it, but the duty to care for the parish community, the lack of spiritual guidance, and the low value placed on the contemplative life within the clergy make it difficult to lead a life of prayer in the modern Western clerical context.

Tantric prayer, on the other hand, impels the practitioner into the experience of emptying kenosis by teaching two subsequent stages that must by necessity follow the stage of purification. Whether in its Taoist, Buddhist, Islamic, or Christian form, the Tantric experience seeks in its second stage to fill the mind with sacred images, to value these images above all others, and then ultimately to empty the mind of all concepts, in order to preserve awareness of transcendent presence. The second or illuminative stage of prayer fills the mind and heart (intellect and will) with images of the sacred from a particular cultural-religious tradition.

For the Christian, as in the *Spiritual Exercises* of St. Ignatius, the stage of purification, a brief week of the month-long prayer experience, is succeeded by two weeks of contemplative envisioning of the life of Jesus. For the Sufi mystic, the sacred words of the Koran, poetic imagery, and sacred dance fill the illuminative process. Tantric Buddhism teaches the two great mandala mediations, the Lotus World (Gharbhadhatu)

### The Gold Pavilion

and the Vajra World (Vajradhatu, Thunder and Lightning, sometimes called Adamantine Mandala).[6] These meditations lead the monk and the laity into the second and third stage of kenotic or "emptying" meditation.

For the religious Taoist, as was seen in chapters 2 and 3, a pure place called Daochang (Tao-ch'ang) is visualized around the meditator. All images within the memory, both good and evil, are sent out of the body before the illuminative stage begins. The meditative ritual for building this sacred place is called *falu*, literally, "lighting the interior alchemical furnace." The meditator uses the palm of the left hand as a mnemonic or remembering device, pressing a joint on the left fingers with the tip of the thumb while emptying out all of the spiritual images and energies from the body. The meditation can be done in a simplified manner by the layperson as follows:

Following the color meditations learned in chapter 3 and in the *Gold Pavilion* meditation, face the north or if in a sacred shrine, chapel, or temple, the sacred image (a crucifix, Buddhist statue, Taoist scroll). Pressing the base of the third or middle finger of the left hand with the tip of the left thumb, see the purple energy from the pineal gland in the upper cinnabar field (center of the head) come forth and rest in the north center of the room. This color represents the primordial gestator of the cosmos. Next press the middle joint of the middle finger and see a gold-yellow light come forth from the heart and rest to the right of the primordial Tao. This figure represents the Tao as a mediator between the inner human body and outer nature. Last, press the tip of the third finger and see a bright white light emanate from the lower cinnabar field (the front of the Gold Pavilion) and come

## Tantric Meditation

to rest to the left of the primordial Tao. This figure represents the Tao as indwelling in the Gold Pavilion. Lao-tzu is seen in this vision.[7]

Next the Taoist empties the five colors out from the five storage organs, as follows. Press the middle joint of the index finger and summon the color blue-green from the liver. Place this aura to the east (the symbol of spring, rebirth, and growth) of your body. The venerable figure of the east in Chinese iconography is Fu Hsi, (Fu Xi) the patron of family life and the home, and the source of the *I Ching*, Book of Changes. Press the tip of the middle finger to summon the red-robed lord of the heart to the south, behind you. Press the middle joint of the fourth (ring) finger to summon the white-robed spirit of the lungs to a spot directly to the west. Finally, press the base of the third finger to bring the dark-robed spirit of the kidneys out, and place him to the northeast (next to the north, where the three primordial spirits are resting). The meditator becomes aware of Tao's inner presence only after emptying all images out of the interior.[8]

An analogous meditation takes place when meditating in the Tantric Buddhist tradition. The Four Guardians, Dhrtarastra in the east, Virudhaka in the south, Virupaksa in the west, and Vaisravana in the north guard the four gateways to the temples of Tibet, China, Korea, and Japan. They also watch over the Lotus World mandala, where Vairocana the Sun Buddha sits in the posture of Zen or Dhyana meditation.[9] These guardian spirits are found as part of the architecture in all Chinese and Tibetan temple structure. The iconography of Christian and Judaic art depicts the archangels Gabriel, Michael, Raphael, and Ariel in similar guardian roles.[10]

The Tantric meditation in which the absolute is encountered takes place in a sacred area guarded by purifying spirits sometimes of violent countenance. This is especially true of the Tibetan spirits. The terrifying forms of Mahakali, Dharamraja, and other protective deities are depicted graphically in temple art.[11]

The figures depict huge blue-, green-, red-, and brown-faced deities robed in animal skins, with belts made of severed human heads and multiple arms laden with weapons of destruction. The weapons are meant to cut from us any remnants of selfishness, impurity, and all obstacles to enlightened union.

The tankas of Tibet, like the Buddhist statues of China, Japan, and southeast Asia, are meant to be used as images invoking the second stage of the mystic prayer of union. As explained again and again by Tibetan religious leaders, the Dalai Lama and the other great rimpoches who have come to the West, the painted or carved image becomes a part of the person who meditates in front of it. The aspects of the Buddha depicted in the picture or carved in the statue are ingested, or breathed into the meditator, and become a part of his or her person through eidetic, creative, living, visualization. The sacred Buddhist or Taoist image is thus not a deity or an idol in front of which the meditator worships. Instead, it is a hidden, subconscious aspect of the self that is made a part of one's conscious person in meditation. The great Asian works of Buddhist art, images of Kuanyin (Guanyin, the bodhisattva Avalokitesvara), Amida, Vairocana, Maitreya (also called Milo), are all meant to be made a part of the meditator's conscious everyday life. The true Buddhist or Taoist devotee becomes the image

*Hayagriva.* Tibetan tanka painting of horse-head Guanyin, one of the twenty-eight manifestations of Avalokitesvara. Tankas are used in Taoist ritual to control and exorcise evil spirits.

projected in meditation, a person filled with compassion, peace, serenity, and healing.

In the practice of the Illuminative Way, the images of peaceful and violent Buddhist deities are seen by the Tibetan nomads, farmers, and many of the monks as deities invoked for favors, healing, and blessing. Tibetan pilgrims circumambulate the temples, turn prayer wheels, prostrate tens of thousands of times before shrines for "merit" (*gongde*), based on the premise that all human deeds (the word *karma* means "deed," not "fate" or "retribution") have cosmic consequences, as cause and effect. Thus past, present, and future deeds can be atoned for by meritorious deeds such as prostrating, circumambulating, chanting the mantric phrase "Om Mani Peme Hum" (Sanskrit: Om Mani Padme Hum, "Om, enlightened by the Lotus, Hum!"). By so chanting, prostrating, and walking, evil is changed into blessing, and the world becomes a "Shambhala," a happy and compassionate place to live.

Though such acts of devotion do not of themselves lead to the prayer of kenosis, in fact the elimination of all conceptual imagery other than the sacred is effected by the Tibetan manner of physical prostration and prayer. The images of the Illuminative Way become the path toward spiritual growth. This process is no more clearly seen than in the great Cham dances of the New Year, the fifteenth of the first lunar month (in the Chinese calendar), fifteen days prior to the Tibetan calendrical New Year. Each temple performs its own Cham dance, maintaining its own manner of performing the dance and its own manner of explanation.[12]

The Cham dance of Labrang temple, on the Gansu-Qinghai border, in northeast Tibet, is one of the most splendid

## Tantric Meditation

and well attended of the New Year performances. A huge fifty by eighty foot tanka painting is "sunned" (unrolled on a hillside) on the day before the Cham, and butter sculptures are displayed on the day after. More than one hundred thousand nomads attend the Labrang temple performance.

The sacred area in front of the main temple of Labrang is laid out for the performance in the following manner. The temple's main entrance is the north side of the square. To the south, about a hundred yards away, is a series of high prayer flags summoning beneficent protective spirits to guard the area. To the right of the prayer flags is prepared a Goma fire altar for burning away all instruments of war and evil, and all impediments to enlightened union. To the west of the sacred area is an altar for food offerings. The musicians, chanters, cymbals, drummers, bone trumpets, and twelve-foot base trumpets are arranged to the east and southeast of the area. All is in readiness by 10:00 A.M., but the first dancers do not appear until noon.

The skeleton dancers come first, then each of the participating deities appear in pairs, the blue-, red-, green-, and brown-faced spirits (Denjema, Gurkor, Turwo, Jenghe, in Amdo dialect), then a blue-faced Mahakali (Dzamenje) and Dharamraja (Chujia, or Enma). The stag and yak dancers also appear, and finally the black-hatted Shanagpa, some thirty in all, who form an extended circle around the sacred area, creating a Vajra (Thunder World) mandala.

The Shanagpa black-hat dancers twirl left and right, then welcome back Mahakali and Dharamraja into the sacred area. The two great kings dance sacred steps that make this present world of illusion into Shambhala, a place where love and wisdom are supreme. After their dance is finished, the lead Shanagpa takes from a large box (offered by a monk) the five instruments of war and destruction, the hammer, hook, trident, Vajra (thunderbolt), and rope. He dances with each of these over his head, one-by-one, replacing each and taking another until all have been held up to the heavens. The weapons of war (purification of evil) are replaced in the box, along with a large cylindrical roll of *dzampa* (an offering of highland roasted barley flour mixed with butter). The *dzampa* represents the lingam of Lord Shiva, that by which the world of illusion was created.[13]

The monk, called Lanka, takes the offerings to the south of the sacred area and lays them in a large pot of oil boiling over the Goma fire. A flask of white alcohol is poured into the oil, which ignites in a huge mushroom cloud of flames, burning away all instruments of war, evil, impurity, and illusion. In these flames are consumed not only all of the illusory world but also the worries, good things, images of the sacred, and the entire illuminative world. Shambhala is a place in which compassion and wisdom are united. Compassion is seen as the male (yang) and wisdom as the female (yin) aspect of reality.

The Cham dance requires five hours to perform, plus almost three hours of waiting, some eight hours in all seated on the hard winter ground in the wind and dust of the Tibetan highlands. Much of the meaning is *sangyak* (Amdo dialect), a part of the oral teaching reserved for the monk initiate. But the meaning grasped by the nomads is clear enough. The great horned Dharamraja, who rules over the punishments of hell, turns this world into a paradise when deeds of compassion are ruled by wisdom. The nomads go back the two or three days by

# Tantric Meditation

bus and on foot to their snowbound pastures, satisfied that for another year their land is blessed and made peaceful by the presence of the great kings of love and wisdom.

It is interesting that in the tanka paintings hanging in the temples, wisdom is always depicted as a woman, and compassion as a man. The two are seen embracing in union, a symbol of the divine and the human made one. Many Westerners interpret these sacred images in a literal sense, that sexual union between monk and consort is a part of the ritual process. This male-chauvinist error is condemned by Lady Wei Huacun (see chapters 3 and 4) and by the monks of Tibet as well, who graphically demonstrate the modern literalist error when burning the lingam of Shiva. Teresa of Ávila in the West, Lady Wei Huacun in fourth-century China, and the Tibetan spiritual masters of the past and today admit only the symbolic meaning of the images, depicted so vividly in temple art.[14]

The Goma fire rite is an external act that illustrates a meditation that takes place internally, within the contemplative life of the practitioner. Just as the *Gold Pavilion* meditation used inner fire and water to wash away all images and desires before realizing inner union with Tao, so the Tantric Buddhist adept burns away all inner visions of the sacred deities, the quiet and peaceful as well as the violent. The philosophy of Tantric Buddhism is the philosophy of emptiness, based on the same sort of nonjudgmental and nonvolitional act taught by the Taoist and other mystic masters. This practical philosophy of emptying is expressed in a very brief passage called the *Heart Sutra*, which is chanted each day by Chinese, Japanese, Korean, and Tibetan monks and laity. A paraphrase of the sutra is as follows:

## The Gold Pavilion

❂

When Avalokitesvara was walking on the shore of deep
> wisdom,

Enlightened, he saw that the five skandhas were
> completely empty.

And thereupon crossed over all sorrow and care.
"O Sariputra, form is not distinct from the empty,
The empty is not distinct from form.
Form is empty, emptiness is form.
Sensation, imagination, judgment, consciousness, too,
> empty.

Sariputra, all dharmas [thoughts] are empty of relation to
> reality,

They are not born or destroyed,
Not sullied or pure, not increased or diminished.
The reason is that the empty [center] has no form,
No sensation, imagination, judgment, or consciousness,
No eyes, ears, nose, tongue, body feelings, or mind
> thoughts,

No color, sound, smell, taste, movement, object of thought,
No world to see, no world to conceive or understand.
No avidya [ignorance] and no end to ignorance,
No old age and death, no escaping old age and death,
No four noble truths [suffering, desire, cessation, path],
No wisdom, nothing attained.
Because nothing is attained, the enlightened rely on
> the shore of wisdom,

And have no snares or obstacles.
Free from snares, they have no fears.
Freed from the world of dream images,
At last they reach Nirvana!

## Tantric Meditation

*All Buddhas of the three time periods [past, now, future]
Rely on wisdom's shore to attain unsurpassed, complete
    awakening.
Therefore realize that the Wisdom Shore is a great spirit
    mantra,
A great bright light mantra,
A supreme, unequalled mantra,
Which can remove all suffering, a true, not false achieve-
    ment.
Therefore let us chant the Wisdom Shore mantra!
It goes like this:
Gone, gone, gone to the other shore!
Arrived at the other shore.
Enlightened! Svaha!*

The union of the meditator with absolute wisdom in the Tantric system, and the union of the Taoist with the transcendent Tao, are both based on a prayer in which judgment and will are suspended. This way of peaceful intuitive union can be easily learned, in any spiritual or cultural context. The dialogue between those who follow the way of emptying and union is also one of few words, much peace, and mutual illumination.

# Notes

## ⊛ Chapter 1

1. See the outline of Taoist history in this chapter for more on the history of Taoism. The reader may refer to a number of translations of the *I Ching* Book of Changes found in modern bookshops for an idea of how the *I Ching* works. The versions of Legge, Wilhelm, Blofeld, and Wu Jingnuan, among many others, are commended.
2. These two works are summarized in chapter 1.
3. John K. Fairbank's and Edwin O. Reischauer's *China: Tradition, and Transformation* (Boston: Houghton Mifflin, 1989); Joseph Needham's *Science and Civilization in China* Volume II (New York: Cambridge University Press, 1956); and Holmes Welch's *Taoism: The Parting of the Way* (Boston: Beacon Press, 1966), follow this opinion.
4. *Ritual* is a term used to translate a number of Chinese words such as *li*, *ji* (*chi*), *jiao*, and *yi* into English. *Li* has a different meaning in the Confucian and the Taoist traditions. For the Confucian it means a stilted form of ceremony used at the courts of the nobles. By derivation it means a set of ceremonial bows and polite formulas used by the noble class at court. By a third derivation, it means politeness, such as is proper to the learned and refined, but not to

## Notes to Chapter One

the lowly and unlearned. The Taoist tradition jokes about this kind of *li*.

For the Taoist *li* means the offering of food, wine, and song when guests or the spiritual energies that represent nature are invoked during festivals. Many of these concepts are taken from the *Liji* (*Li-chi,* or Record of Rites); based on yin-yang philosophy, it is a second-century B.C.E. work used by the Confucian and Taoist traditions alike. This kind of ritual is associated with Chinese rites of passage such as birthing, marriage, healing, and burial.

*Ji* means the offering at festivals of sacrificial items such as food, wine, and song to the invisible spirit elements of nature. Chinese offer rites of this kind for the seasonal changes in nature.

*Jiao* (*chiao*) means the offering of wine and incense during all festivals that celebrate life, such as weddings, building dedications, and village renewals, and when meditating on the Tao of nature. *Jiao* ritual acts out the ideas of the *Lao-tzu* and *Chuang-tzu* classics in symbolic drama.

*Yi* refers to state rituals, religious sacrifices, and all other ceremonies where a liturgical master, priest, or other expert is required. The words *li* and *yi* have almost the same meaning and are sometimes used together.

5. The word *shen* is the standard Chinese term for spirit. The word *ling* refers to a spiritual quality. The soul itself is thought to have two sets of functions, the *hun* or yang functions of intellect, will, and intuition, and the *p'o* or yin functions that govern the feelings and emotions. From ancient times the Chinese believed that the spirit of *shen* exists after death. After being alchemically purified in a hell-purgatory that restores yin-yang balance, it then "ascends to the heavens," leaving the range of human memory. An orphaned soul with no descendants to remember it during festivals is a *guei,* a demonic or unrequited angry soul.

6. Note that the Confucian system keeps spirits at a distance. *Jing gui*

## Notes to Chapter One

*shen er yuan ji*, "Respect the demons and spirits, but keep a safe distance," is a Confucian ideal.

7. See chapter 4.

8. At the time of receiving the register, one is also given a Taoist title, a name (with one of forty or more characters in a poem indicating the source of the master's learning), a talisman, and other paraphernalia showing the authenticity of one's register and ordination. A similar ritual is followed in the ordination of a Buddhist monk in the Tibetan and Japanese Tantric traditions. See Saso, M., *Dokyo Hiketsu Shusei* (Tokyo: Ryukei Shosha, 1979) for lists of various Taoist registers still used in modern China.

9. The so-called *Tao of Sex*, which is used by some Western therapists in marriage counseling, is preserved in sections of the official Taoist canon, as are many other extraneous texts from a variety of non-Taoist sources. The practice of *fangzhong* (suppressing the flow of semen in the male or orgasm in the female during the sex act) is based on the false notion that losing semen causes early death and saving semen promotes long life. The "saved" semen is in fact passed out through the urethra when next urinating. The grossly male-chauvinist act of having sex an endless number of times with many women or maintaining prolonged erection has no known health benefits in medicine, other than bolstering the male ego. The practice was condemned by the female Taoist Lady Wei Huacun in the early fourth century, and again by the male Taoist Kou Qianzhi (K'ou Ch'ien-chih) at a later date. Those who practice it are not given a Taoist *lu* register or license of ordination.

10. This definition is taken from the *Chuang-tzu Nei-p'ien*, chapters 4 and 5, the terms *zuowang* (*tso-wang*, "sitting in forgetfulness"), and *xinzhai*, (*hsin-chai*, fasting in the heart). See chapter 2 for an explanation of these methods.

11. Tibetan oracles, Mongol and Korean shamans, southeast and southwest China's mediums, and the Redhat priest are the subject of a separate study now in progress by the author.

## Notes to Chapter One

12. Fairbank's and Reishchauer's *China: Tradition, & Transformation*, and Arthur Cotterell's *China: A Concise Cultural History* (New York: NAL-Dutton, 1990) provide a good beginning (with bibliography) for those who want to read more about the Confucian tradition.
13. The *I Ching* consists of sixty-four brief oracular statements, each followed by six "wings" or longer explanations of what the oracle means. The wings are of very late composition, probably 200 B.C.E. and after. The sixty-four opening oracles have no mention of iron-age metal implements and may have been composed before 1100 B.C.E.
14. Lao-tzu supposedly lived in the sixth to the fifth century B.C.E. and was visited and respected by Confucius. Most scholars agree that the present text seems to have been written out by his followers at a later date. More than two hundred translations of this work are available in English paperback editions.
15. A modern cartoon book, available in Chinese and English, probably comes closest to capturing its spirit. For good modern translations see the works in print of Burton Watson and the late Angus Graham.
16. The spread of the Redhat tradition is not limited to the Han Chinese. The Yao, Miao, Yi, Naxi, and other minority ethnic groups of southwest China were deeply influenced by and in turn affected the popular Redhat exorcism and healing rituals. This is especially true of the Yunnan Province in southwest China. The Dongba rites of the Naxi, the Daba rites of the Muosuo, the ritual manuals of the Yao, the Ngapa and Bonpo rites of Tibet are analogous in many cases to the Redhat tradition of southeast China. The sinification of southeast China, that is, the cultural conquest and assimilation by the Chinese of the native groups of the southern provinces of Jejiang, Fujian, Gwangdong, Gwangxi, and Hunan, and other parts of the south, may account for the unmistakable similarities between the ethnic minority cultures of the south and the newly evolved southern Song dynasty culture. The

# Notes to Chapter Two

ethnic groups of southwest China in Gwangxi, Guizhou, and Yunnan borrowed from and deeply influenced Redhat ritual. Lao-tzu became a benign spirit, the same "Laozhun" (Lord Lao-tzu) patron of the Redhat ritual tradition.

17. The term *mijue* (mi-chueh) refers to a hand-copied manual, given by a Taoist master to his or her disciple, that explains the meditative or ritual use of a classical Taoist text. The manual used here derives from Taoist Lady Wei Huacun and the Mao Shan Shang-ch'ing tradition. It is used today in the Shangqing (Shang-ch'ing), Qingwei (Ch'ing-wei), and Quanzhen (Ch'uan-chen) schools mentioned earlier.

## Chapter 2

1. Qi (ch'i) is a word commonly used in Chinese and Japanese. It can mean primordial energy, such as in the scientific sense of atomic energy; life energy in plants, animals, and humans; and breath, as when one breathes in oxygen. The primordial Tao in this passage is seen to give birth to all three kinds of *qi*.
2. Put in terms of modern medical research, our bodies secrete a certain amount of hormones and other body-restoring elements when we sleep. One of these is melatonin, a hormone that begins to restore energy when we pass from ordinary consciousness into the *alpha state* (the left and right lobes of the brain beating in harmony at less than twelve beats per second), then the *theta state* (six beats), and into sleep. When one performs the nonjudgmental qi meditations of the Taoist tradition, the alpha state is almost immediately reached. In meditation the body rebuilds itself and thus maintains health. The Taoists assign the color purple to what modern science calls the melatonin complex, and thus meditate on "purple" to restore primordial breath.
3. The meditation of centering is explained more fully in chapter 4.
4. One of the signs of a Taoist kingdom is that the lame, crippled, out-

## Notes to Chapter Two

cast, and needy come there. Confucius avoided the lame and physically deformed. Chuang-tzu makes these the men and women of greatest virtue.

5. The text is sometimes translated, sometimes summarized and paraphrased.
6. The great fish Kun is a symbol of yin, and the great bird Peng is yang. The six months of Kun's journey in the water represents the six months of yin's domination in nature: autumn and winter. At the end of this period yin's dominance gives way and the great fish becomes the great bird, who flies off to the heavens, that is, spring and summer in nature.
7. Yao was one of the three great sage kings of ancient China, whose name occurs in the Outline of Taoist History in chapter 1. Confucius used these three kings as models of the good ruler blessed by heaven. Chuang-tzu here borrows the image and makes Yao into a Taoist sage-king.
8. This passage is cited again at the beginning of King Tai's Response to Tao. Wangyi was asked four questions by Yuejue.
9. *Xinzhai* or heart fasting is one of the two basic Taoist techniques of meditation. The other is *zuowang*, "sitting in forgetfulness." It is to be noted that in both cases Chuang-tzu puts the explanation of "heart fasting" and "sitting in forgetfulness" into the mouth of Confucius. In both cases Confucius teaches the method at the request of Yan Hui, a Confucian disciple.
10. The word *fu* for a talismanic contract is used here in the Chinese text, in the sense of uniting the two halves of a talisman. The *fu* in ancient China was a contract of loyalty made between the king and his knights or ministers on the one hand, and between the king and heaven on the other. The image here is of a *fu* contract made between Tao and the heart. The Tao and the heart are joined into one, as the two halves of a talisman are joined to prove loyalty between king and his knights.
11. The altar to the *she* spirit of the crops and soil is always put under the branches of a large gnarled tree. These trees with their shrines

## Notes to Chapter Three

are often preserved in modern China. The shrines have been turned into sundry goods stores for tourists, altars to the spirit of consumerism that now rules modern socialist China as it does in the capitalist West.

12. In ancient China young women were sometimes offered as live sacrifices to rivers in spring, to ask for blessing from the river spirit. Then a wise king of Chu in the south ordered that only the daughters of priests and shamans be used for the sacrifice. From that year on, it was recorded, human sacrifices ended.

13. For those who look at the Chinese text, the word *xia* in the ancient version should be read with the jade radical *xia* for veins or distinctions, rather than with the man radical *jia* for error. The passage is quoted from the second-century B.C.E. *Huainanzi*, the "Jingshen" chapter, with this poetic variation.

14. See *Tao-te Ching*, chapter 71, and the Meditation on Not Knowing in this chapter.

15. Note that *Taiji* is the same as primordial *qi* breath, *hundun* the demiurge or chaos in chapter 7 of the *Chuang-tzu*, and *yuwei ji dao*, the immanent Tao or nature mother, who spins forth breath in chapter 6 of the *Tao-te Ching*.

16. East, south, west, north, and the two directions of center and up and down.

17. See chapter 3.

18. Empty Gourd demonstrates here four of the nine stages of emptying meditation. See chapter 3 for later Taoist meditations on this passage.

19. Taoists still call ritual meditations that bring about union with Tao "getting drunk on peace," *zui taiping*.

## ❂ Chapter 3

1. The teaching that color, sound, and image can be used to "blind" the mind and turn the heart from worldly or selfish pursuits is common to the Taoist and the Tantric Buddhist traditions. In both sys-

## Notes to Chapter Three

tems body, mouth, and mind are used together in synchronicity to bring about immediate awareness of the transcendent experience. Mudra hand dance, mantra chant, and mandala meditation from a cosmic center are common to both systems.

2. The breathing meditation is in fact a quiet, meditative way of doing tai chi exercise. The word *t'ai-chi* (*taiji*) in fact means primordial breath, the Great First Principle of *qi* energy gestated by Tao. "Tao gives birth to One" (*Tao-te Ching*, chapter 42) is translated as "Tao gives birth to t'ai-chi" in many Taoist texts. The second step in the meditation shows how to focus on *taiji*, primordial breath.

3. See *Tao-te Ching*, chapters 22 and 23.

4. The so-called lotus mudra (hand symbol), the open right palm laid on top of the open left palm, placed palms upward in the lap with the tips of the left and right thumbs touching, is a simple way of representing the centering position.

5. A point 1.1618 or 8/5 off center, as seen in the curvature of the chambered nautilus, a horse's hoof, and a deer's antler, and precisely the location just beneath the navel or umbilical cord in humans, represents a true fulcrum or balancing point in nature.

6. Many statues and paintings in Chinese, Japanese, Tibetan, and other Asian sacred places depict ferocious guardian spirits who have eyes looking out through a shield on the stomach. The idea that the intuitive powers "see" directly through gut-feeling awareness is a universally recognized symbol.

7. The Buddhist Samatha-vipasyana meditation is quite similar to the Taoist centering process. The difference in the two systems is the Taoist use of color and sound to empty the place of centering attention. The Chinese word for Samatha-vipasyana, *zhiguan* (*chih-kuan*), means "cessation" (*zhi*) of the mind and will, followed by "contemplation" (*guan*), looking outward. In both systems the lower belly is the place from which looking outward (*guan*) takes place.

8. The term gut feelings in English, along with similar terms in other Indo-European, Semitic, Altaic, Pacific, Native American, and

## Notes to Chapter Three

African languages, bears the universal sense of a kind of knowledge not mediated by the formation of a preconceived image, formal concept, or spoken word. Intuition refers to an experience that precedes word or formal logic but is nonetheless accurate.

9. It is not peculiar to the Chinese system alone that head, heart, and belly are considered to be the abodes of intellect, will, and intuitive feeling. These ideas are found in the tanka paintings of Tibetan Buddhism and the mystic symbols of Cabala and Sufi mysticism. Taoist texts teach the novice that the five *zang* organs are where the intellect, will, emotions, feelings, and intuition "rest," whereas the upper, center, and lower cinnabar fields (head, chest, belly) are their respective offices or working places. The next chapter will show how these various areas are alchemically "refined" by the warming flames and cooling waters of interior meditation. The meditator becomes aware of the power of the lower cinnabar field to intuit the peaceful nonchanging aspects of nature. This newfound power to meditate is at first used to circulate healing colors and sounds within the self, thus purifying and healing the mind and heart of its worries and ills.

10. *Tao-te Ching*, chapter 13.

11. *Chuang-tzu*, chapter 7, as quoted in chapter 2 of this book.

12. Note the similarity here to the teachings of the two great Western mystics, John of the Cross (Juan de la Crúz) and Teresa of Ávila. The Christian "dark night of the intellect and dark night of the senses" find parallels in Taoist centering and Buddhist Madhyamika "nonjudgment" texts as well as in Tibetan Tantric rites of fire emptying.

13. The use of drugs is absolutely forbidden in meditation. For the person who practices centering, drugs in any form impede the intuitive ability to be aware of the reality of the outer world. Hallucinogenic drugs pattern mind images by imposing figures from within the brain, giving the illusion of a heightened awareness of reality. The sense of peace and calm achieved by the centering process so far excels the high of drugs as to allow the

## Notes to Chapter Three

drug experience to be felt for what it really is, no more than chemically induced schizophrenia.

14. The importance of color in Tantric Tibetan and other forms of Buddhist art is analogous to the Taoist use of color described here. The symbolic use of color is perennial and universal. For successful visualization the colors must be pleasantly bright, rather than dull or garish. The colors take the place of envisioning spirits, practiced by the ordained Taoist priest and Tantric Buddhist monk.

15. The choice of key or tone used to initiate a meditative chant does not depend so much on the time of day as the kind of chant being sung. The Taoist musician uses the tone that corresponds to the melody being used to chant a text. The text itself is called a Morning, Noon, or a Night Audience with the Tao, but the melodies and meditative colors used with the accompanying meditation are very many. The meditations of Taoists and Tantric Buddhist monks use body or hand dance (mudra), the intonation of meditative mantras (sounds for which the tone rather than the meaning is important), and the visualization of patterned colors (a mandala or centered meditation) in a manner that coordinates body, mouth, and mind in prayer. Sound, motion, and color bring the whole body into a centered meditation. In this form of prayer it is important to realize that the whole body takes part in the meditation. See the explanations of Tantric prayer in chapter 5.

16. The Taoist, shaman, and Tantric Buddhist traditions all use this visualization process to cleanse the body of "impure green" illness. The color green, like fresh grass in spring, is seen to restore a body tired out from worry and anxiety. The powerful Tibetan Tantric version of the meditation sees the color bright green as a tear coming from the left eye of Avalokitesvara (Kuanyin, or Chenrezi, the bodhisattva of compassion), which turns into the healing spirit Green Tara. A white-colored tear from the right eye becomes the compassionate White Tara.

17. The middle joint of the index finger is a meditation access point or meridian that connects to the liver, the direction east, the season

## Notes to Chapter Three

spring, and the color green in Taoist ritual meditation. Pressing this spot heals the body of fatigue.

18. When envisioned as a bright red flame it can also be evoked to give courage and a sense of spiritual protection for the meditator. The wrathful deities of Tibetan and Japanese Tantric Buddhism, such as the red face of Mahakala and the crimson flames around Acala (Fudo Myoo), purify the meditator of any sullying feelings of anger, pride, and vengeance.

19. Many do this meditation when actually bathed in the rays of the sun. Taoist, Tibetan Buddhist, and Qigong masters use the hands to "bathe" the body in sunlight. The use of body together with mind and imagination increases the effect of the meditation. Others prefer simply to imagine the process.

20. The modern term *alpha state* refers to a condition wherein the left and right lobes of the brain, when measured electronically, are seen to pulsate in harmony at a low rate. This condition brings about a feeling of peace, enhances awareness of the outer world, and excretes the restorative hormone melatonin into the body. Meditating for thirty minutes or so in alpha state refreshes the body as much as if not more than sleep. The Taoists believe that performing this meditation brings good health and impedes aging.

21. Bright yellow-gold is a universal symbol of healing and protection. The use of gold foil to cover a Buddhist statue, a chalice used to celebrate Catholic Mass, gifts of gold jewelry that show love and the natural blessing of wealth, are examples of the symbolic use of gold to protect, honor the sacred, and bring blessing.

22. Many of the rites of tropical Africa and South America use three major colors, white (birth), red (maturation), and black (death), in religious ritual. On closer examination, these three colors in fact include a manifold spectrum of shades. Red includes pink, yellow, and orange; and black diffuses into shades of purple, blue, and green in ritual and art. Culture assigns analogous meaning to color that, in any case, is comparable and analogous.

Notes to Chapter Four

## ⊛ Chapter 4

1. The *liu-ting* (*liuding*) six lady spirits represent the purifying powers of yin within the body that protect and keep the heart free from impure desires. Their opposites are the *liu-chia* (*liujia*), male yang spirits that bring death and destruction. See Michael Saso, *The Teachings of Taoist Master Chuang* (New Haven: Yale University Press, 1978), chapter 4, for a description of the six chia spirits.

## ⊛ Chapter 5

1. *The Spiritual Exercises* of Ignatius of Loyola teach the meditator to kneel, stand, sit, and walk during meditation. An annotation suggests that the adept be continually aware of divine presence, a lifelong form of spiritual practice.
2. The Pure Land method of chanting Buddhist sutras is meant, like Zen, to purify the mind of images and the heart of desires, thus fulfilling the third step of the Buddha's fourfold path. The four noble truths of Buddhism are; all of human life is conditioned by suffering; suffering is caused by selfish desire; the annihilation of selfish images/desires leads to enlightening peace; and once this peace is attained the rest of one's life is lived in selfless compassion (love) for others. The third step, of emptying the mind of judgment and the heart of desires, is a kenotic form of practice. All of the Buddhist prayer methods, whether concentration of the mind (Zen, Chan, Dhyana), chant, or total body prayer (Tantric prayer) are meant to fulfill the third noble truth. The use of chant for "merit" or for awakening an act of pure faith in the saving power of Amida are later developments in the Mahayana (Great Vehicle) forms of Chinese and Japanese Buddhism. See the excellent works of Al Bloom and Tai Unno on Shinran and Tannisho, respectively, for this late Japanese form of "Pure Faith" Buddhism.
3. The Senoi tribe of central Malaysia are noted for having had no known crime for four hundred years, until the coming of Islam and

## Notes to Chapter Five

Christian missionaries with the values of consumer society and money profit. The matriarchal Muosuo of Lugu Lake in northwest Yunnan Province, China, devout followers of Gelugpa and an earlier Kagyupa Tantric Buddhism, also have no known history of crime or violence, and have refused all modernization, electricity, or the use of motor boats in Lugu Lake. The Muosuo claim that the devout practice of Tantric Buddhism accounts for their peaceful way of life.

4. See Evelyn Underhill, *Mysticism*; Ignatius of Loyola, *The Spiritual Exercises*; and Gregory of Nyssa, *Migne Patrology*, for Western accounts of this process. The structural analysis of Ndembu African ritual by the late Victor Turner gives an excellent example of African ritual use of color involving white for purification, red for illumination, and black for the step into the absolute. See Victor Turner, *The Anthropology of Religion*, vol. 3, (London: Tavistock, 1965).
5. Note the use of fire and water symbols in the *Gold Pavilion* text in this regard. Taoist and Buddhist rites begin with the lighting of incense (fire) and sprinkling of water for purification.
6. See Michael Saso, *Tantric Art and Meditation: The Tendai Tradition* (Honolulu: University of Hawaii Press, 1990), for a simplified version of these two meditations in the Japanese Tendai tradition. The complete version of the text with Siddham Sanskrit mantras is published by the Scholar's Press, Delhi, 1990.
7. See Michael Saso, *The Teachings of Taoist Master Chuang* (New Haven: Yale University Press, 1978).
8. The *fa lu* is more complicated in its ritual form. The reader is referred to note 7 above for a fuller explanation.
9. See Saso, *Tantric Art and Meditation*, the *Lotus Mandala*, pp. 34, 65–66, for these figures. The gates of the Lotus Mandala are locked and sealed from all external influence during the meditation of Samatha awareness.
10. The visions of Isaiah and Ezekiel and those in the book of Revelation are biblical examples of protective spirits guarding sacred meditative or visionary areas.

### Notes to Chapter Five

11. The restored temples of Qinghai and Gansu provinces (part of Greater Tibet) are accessible sources for studying these remarkable figures. The red-faced Mahakala and blue countenance of Mahakali stare down at pilgrims and tourists who ride train, then bus from Beijing via Lanzhou and Xining into the Tibetan temples of Northeast Tibet. Labrang temple at Xiaho in Gansu, Rongwo temple in Tongren (Rekong) and Kumbun temple (known in Chinese as Ta-er Si, a bus ride from Xining city in Quinghai) have been restored and are open to pilgrims and visitors as in the past. The temples and households of a village to the east of Rekong city (Huangnan) are dedicated to painting Tibetan style Buddhist images known as tanka. Older versions of tanka paintings, rescued by the farmers and nomads from the destruction of the Cultural Revolution, are for sale in the open markets of Labrang and Kumbun (Ta-er Si). These religious art works from the past can be purchased at a fraction of the price asked for in Hongkong and western markets, where they are sold to museums and art collectors for public exhibition.
12. The Cham dancers, called Chambawa, require three years of training and nine years of performing before becoming masters. The meaning of the Cham, its preparation, and its intricate dance steps are taught in private within the temple precincts for six to eight weeks before the performance. Cham dances are performed on the fifteenth day of the first, fourth, and seventh lunar months in most Tibetan temples. Thousands of nomads and farmers come down from the high grasslands to participate.
13. The Indian antecedents of Tantric Buddhism considered Lord Shiva (represented by the lingam) and his consort Lady Wisdom to be the gestators and destroyers of the world of judgment. By burning Shiva's lingam, the world of illusion that impedes enlightenment, as well as all of the images of the sacred, is burned away.
14. The tanka used here as illustrations are taken from Mongol as well as ancient and modern Tibetan sources.

✱ APPENDIX

# A COMPARATIVE CHART OF TAOIST HISTORY

| | | |
|---|---|---|
| 1100–800 B.C.E | • The 64 opening lines of the *I-Ching (Yijing)* Book of Changes | • Homer's *Iliad* and *Odyssey*, Moses in Egypt, Exodus |
| 600–300 B.C.E | • Confucius, Lao-tzu, Chuang-tzu; the Warring States in China | • Socrates, Plato, Aristotle, Alexander the Great |
| 200 B.C.E–200 C.E. | • The first Chinese empire; religious Taoism develops | • The Roman Empire; Christianity founded |
| 300–500 | • Buddhism comes to China; Taoist mystic Wei Huacun | • Christianity comes to Europe |
| 600–900 | • Confucian, Buddhist, Taoist: three teachings, one culture | • Islamic, Judaic, and Christian, three cultures |
| 900–1000 | • The religious reformation in China, laity meditate | • Medieval Christianity, monks and nuns meditate |
| 1300–1600 | • Mongol conquest; the Ming dynasty succeeds in China; tai-chi and kung fu martial arts begin | • 16th century religious reform; western mystic Teresa of Ávila |
| 1600–1900 | • Western missionaries, then colonial occupation come to Asia; Japan modernizes | • Intellectual, industrial, social revolutions in the West |
| 1900–present | • Marxist social revolution then modernization come to China; rebirth of religion. | • Asian meditation and Buddhist/Asian dialogue come to the West |

While Chinese culture maintained a continuity over the last three millennia, the civilizations of Europe, northern Africa, and the Near and Middle East underwent continual and drastic changes. Taoism, a way of life rather than a religious belief system, remains throughout this period at the core of Chinese ascetic and interior practice.

# Glossary and Index of Special Terms

## A

the **absolute** xii, 156, 160, 167, see **transcendent Tao**, *wuwei chih tao*

**Acala** (Fudo Myoo) 179, Tantric Buddhist Spirit of fire purification

**Aidaido** 59, a sage of the Zhuangzi Taoist tradition

**alpha state** 95, 137, 173, 179, a quiet state of meditation, in which brain pulses are less than twelve beats per second

**Amida** 160, the Buddha who saves all sentient beings upon invoking his name

**Ao** a great fish, symbol of yin, in the depths of the Taoist ocean

**apophasis** 12, 25, 41, the prayer of emptiness, in which mind and will are stilled

**apophatic prayer** xi, 9, 11, 12, 23, 25, 41, 75, see above

**apophatic symbol** 75

**Avalokitesvara** (Chn. Kuanyin, Jpn. Kannon, Tbt. Chenrezi) 160, 166, 178, the Bodhisattva of compassion

*avidya* 166, ignorance

## B

**Baiyun-Guan** xiv, 23, White Cloud Taoist Temple, Beijing

*Baopuzi* (Pao-p'u Tzu) 22, an early Taoist book published by Go Hong, in 317 C.E. The title *Gold Pavilion* appears in this manual.

*The Gold Pavilion*

❀

**Big Dipper** (*Beidou, Pei-tou*) 63, 95, 112, 116, 130, 131, a constellation in the northern heavens symbolizing prayer centered on Tao

**Blackhat** (*Wutou*) 8, 9, Taoists of the Zheng yi school who perform burial rites as well as meditation on the Tao (distinguish *shanagpa*, Tibetan black-hat Cham ritual dancers)

**bodhisattva** (*pusa*) a person who, once enlightened, vows to save all sentient beings; also a term used in colloquial Chinese for a small statue

**Bonpo** 172, (also, *Bon*) ancient Tibetan religion. Elements of Bon are preserved in the Nakhi Dongba rites today

**breath energy** 82, (see *qi, ch'i*); the mind directs the flow of energy through the body in Taoist qigong meditation, and in Wushu martial arts.

## C

**Cabala** 177, the Jewish meditative tradition, and Islamic Sufi practice, contain elements similar to Taoist prayer

**Cham dances** 162–64, 182, Tibetan Buddhist ritual in which meditative visualization is acted out in sacred dance

**Chambawa** 182, Tibetan Buddhist dancers

**ch'ang-sheng** (*changsheng*) 114, 127, 146, long life, or in meditation, Tao generating qi energy in the Gold Pavilion

**chen** (*zhen*) true, Tao realized

**chen** (*zhen*) 124, 130, 131, one of the four mantic words used in the *I Ching*; to prognosticate, rest, pure, meditate place of central focus during meditation

**Chengi** (*zhengyi*) 125, 150 "True One" Taoist school of Chang Tao-ling, from Dragon-tiger Mountain, southeast China

**cheng-shih** (*zhengshi*) 115, another name for the Gold Pavilion, the place of central focus during meditation.

**chen-jen** (*zhenren*) 110, 127, a Tao-realized person in the Chuang-tzu meditative tradition

**Chenrezi** 178, Tibetan for Avalokitesvara, the Bodhisattva of compassion

**ch'i breath** (qi) 100, 101, passim, see **breath energy, qi**

**chiang-kung** (*jianggong*) 132, acupuncture point, also "red palace," symbolic name for the heart

# Glossary and Index of Special Terms

❀

**Chiao rites** 4, 131, 170, Taoist ritual meditation for cosmic and interior renewal

***ch'ien*** (qian) 112, 121, 122, 129, passim, the first of the eight trigrams, symbol of pure yang, heaven; three unbroken lines

***ch'ih-t'a*** (chita) 112, the Gold Pavilion as empty, a "foot long" palace waiting for the presence of the Tao; note the variable meaning of the text

***ch'ih-tzu*** (chizi) 131, the hierophant or ruddy child gestated within the Gold Pavilion when Tao is present

***ch'i-kuan*** (qiguan) 104, 176, the passage way of primordial qi into the Gold Pavilion during meditation

***ch'i-kung*** meditative exercise for nourishing and increasing qi energy within the body (see **qigong**)

***ching*** (jing) 100, 102, passim, the power of intuition, located in the lower cinnabar field; the emotions; semen; yin energy

**Ch'ing-wei (Qingwei) Taoism** 22, *wu-lei fa* thunder rites, shared with Tantric Buddhist practices of Tibet

***ch'u*** 122, the portal that leads from the Gold Pavilion, that is, the yang or *qian* entrance to meditation

**Ch'üan-chen (Quanzhen) Taoism** 23, 110, the "All True" reformed Taoist school; see **Baiyun-Guan, Beijing**

**Chüan Hsü** (*Zhuanxu*) 14, 109, Taoist spirit who rules over the northern skies and the kidneys in the Taoist body

**Chuang-tzu** 4, passim, the 350 B.C.E. Taoist sage whose *Chuang-tzu Nei-p'ien* is the standard meditation manual for classical Taoist prayer

**Chuang-tzu Nei-p'ien** 3–4, passim, the first seven chapters of the work attributed to the Taoist sage Chuang-tzu

***ch'ui-hung*** 117, another term for the North Star

***chung-lou*** (*zhonglou*) 132, acupuncture point used as a reference for Taoist meditation

**Chung tan-t'ien** (*zhong dantian*) 79, 144, the central cinnabar field, i.e., the heart, in Taoist meditation

***chu-shen*** (*zhushen*) 144, the spirit of the heart, master of all the spirits in the body

**Confucianism** 1, 15, passim

**Confucius** (*K'ung-tsu*, Kongzi) 14, 50, 51, 53, 58, 64, 172, 174, the

*187*

great teacher of ancient China, who defined and taught the basic rules of social relationships

# D

**Daba** 172, ancient Bon rites of Tibet, preserved by the Muosuo people of the Yunnan-Tibet-Siquan border

***Daode Jing*** see ***Tao-te Ching***

**Daojia** (*Tao-chia*) 4, a follower of the Lao-tzu *Tao-te Ching*, a school of philosophers in B.C.E. China

**Daojiao** (*Tao-chiao*) 4, religious Taoism, and one of its many schools, dating from the late Han dynasty (2nd century C.E.)

*daoshi* (Tao-chih) 7, 9, 11, a Taoist priest

*de* (te) 59, virtue, power, the immanent Tao of motion, t'ai-chi

**Denjema** (Tbt.) 163, a Tibetan *Yidam* protective spirit

**Dharamraja** (Chn. Yenluo Wang, Jpn. Enma, Amdo Tbt., Chujia) 160, 163, 164, the Tantric Buddhist ruler of hell

**dharma** (Chn. Fa, Jpn. Ho) 166, the Buddhist way, Buddha's teachings

**Dhrtarastra** xii, 159, guardian spirit of the east; one of the Four Heavenly kings who stand at the entrance of Buddhist temples

**Dhyana** (Chn. *chan*, Jpn. *Zen*) 154, 159, 180, meditation for calming the mind

*di* 51, the Chinese word for the highest deity, the heavenly equivalent for the **Huang Ti** visible ruler on earth

*ding xin* v, to quiet or empty the heart and mind of thoughts and desires

**Dongba** 172, ancient Bon rituals of Tibet preserved by the Nakhi people of Lijiang, Yunnan; see **Daba**

**Dragon-Tiger Taoism** 14, 15, 21, 95, the Zhengyi Lunghu Shan school of Taoism

*du* **channel** 83, the passage of qi energy from the base of the spine to the top of the head, and down to the mouth (see **ren channel**)

**dzampa** 164, highland parched barley flour used as a staple diet in Tibet

# Glossary and Index of Special Terms

## E

**earth** passim, center of the outer cosmos, corresponding to the chest of the inner cosmos, the human body

## F

*fa* 109, dharma, Buddhist teaching, the power of the Buddha's teaching (and perforce Taoist practice)

*falu* 158, 181, a list of spirit's names, their mantric commands, talismans and images to be summoned during Taoist meditation

*fang-ts'un* (*fangcun*) 106, 107, the empty space in the center of the Gold Pavilion in which the hierophant is conceived when Tao is present

*fangzhong* (*fang-chung*) 8, 171, sexual hygiene i.e., the suppression of semen in order to preserve male vigor. The practice is condemned in actual Taoist practice

*fashi* 9, 11, a redhat or popular healer as opposed to a *Daoshi* Taoist master

**fasting in the heart-mind** see **xinzhai**

**five phase system** (*yinyang wuxing*) 4, 71, another name for yin-yang five element cosmology

*fu* 57, 104, 105, 174, a talisman, or talismanic contract with a spirit, energy of nature

*fu* 74, 134, 139, 141, one of the six organs of the lower abdomen; i.e., *liu fu*

**Fu Hsi** (Fu Xi) xii, 13, 109, 159, the spirit patron of the East, primordial human being, creator of the sixty-four hexagrams

## G

**Gharbhadhatu** (*Gharbadhatu*) (Chn. Taizang jie, Jpn. Taizo Kai) 157, the Womb or Lotus World mandala; see **Vajra Dhatu**

**the Gold Pavilion** [concept] 24, 99, 100, passim, a void center in the microcosm (human body) wherein the Tao dwells

**the *Gold Pavilion* classic** (Chn. *Huang-t'ing Ching*) ix, passim, a canonical text

**Goma fire** 163, 165, Sanskrit *Agni Hottra*, a ritual for burning away all impediments to enlightenment, transcendent union

*gongde* 162, meritorious human acts

**Gozao Shan** 22, sacred Taoist mountain in southeast China

**the Great Abyss** see *t'ai-yüan*

**the Great Tao** (*wuwei chih tao*, *wuwei zhi dao*) 147

**the Great Ultimate** (*T'ai-chi*, *Taiji*) 63

**the Great Void** 114, where Tao dwells

**the Great Yin** 143, 146, mother Tao gestating primordial breath

*guan* 176, looking outward

**Guanyin** see **Kuanyin**

*guei* 170, a demon or demonic spirit

**Gurkor** 163, a *Yidam* or protective spirit of Tibetan Buddhism

**Guyi mountains** 43, 44, 49, a place cited in the Chuang-tzu where sages and immortals dwell

# H

*hai-yüan* 109, a Taoist meditative term for the kidneys

**heart fasting** (Chn. *xinzhai*) 24, 52, 54, 89, 174, a term from Chuang-tzu, chapter 4; the cessation of judgment and desire as preludes to union with Tao

**heart-mind** (Chn. *xin*, *hsin*) 66, passim, the word *xin* in Chinese refers to all activities of mind and heart, i.e., knowing and willing

**Heart Sutra** 165

**heaven** (Chn. *tian*, *t'ien*), 28, 31, passim, the highest section of the three-layered cosmos, corresponding to the human head

**heaven's gate** (Chn. *Tianmen*) 134, 138, 140, the trigram *qian*, the northwest direction

**heng** 124, 131, a word from the *I Ching* Book of Changes, second of the four mantic words *yüan*, *heng*, *li*, *chen*, to sacrifice, nest, nurture

**Highest Pure school** (Chn. Shangqing Pai) ix, 22, 25, 151, the Taoist meditative tradition, *Gold Pavilion* teachers

*hoatsu* 9, Taiwanese pronunciation for the term *fashi*, a Redhat healer

## Glossary and Index of Special Terms

***ho-t'u*** (hotu) 122, 125, 133, 143, the River Chart, a term for the magic chart used by Yü the Great to stop the floods in ancient China; the paraphernalia of a ruler; a set of Talismans used by Taoists to renew the cosmos

***hou*** 124, a twenty minute period of time in meditation practice. A minimum of Two *hou* are suggested as an ideal time period

***hou-t'ien*** (houtian) 103, 125, the eight trigrams of King Wen, which represent change in the cosmos

***hsia-chi*** 111, 132, 149, acupuncture point on the back of the skull, used as a reference in meditation

***hsien-t'ien*** (*xiantian*) 103, 122, 125, 133, the prior heavens, the eight trigrams of Fu Hsi, the unchanging aspects of Tao in the cosmos

***hsin-chai*** 27, see ***xinzhai***

***hsü*** 117, the empty heart-mind

***hsüan*** 102, the yang, male entrance to the Gold Pavilion

***hsüan-ch'i*** 148, Tao as principle working in the cosmos

***hsüan-ch'uan*** 132, Tao as source of qi being gestated in the cosmos

***hsüan-ying*** 104, the upper rib cage

***hu*** 139, to breathe

***hua*** 49, change, transformation; distinguish hua for flower

***hua-ch'ih*** 135, 136, flowery pool, the kidneys

***Huainanzi*** (*Huai-nan-tzu*) 66, 2nd-century B.C.E. manual of Taoist lore

***hua-kai*** 135, 138, 139, 141, rib cage, upper chest

**Huang Ti** (Huangdi) 13, 109, Yellow Emperor, spirit patron of the Center, earth, (stomach-spleen)

**Huangnan** 149, a Tibetan district in Qinghai south of Lake Kokonor

**Huang-t'ing Ching** (***Huangting Jing***) 6, 22, the Gold Pavilion Classic

**Huang-t'ing Nei-ch'ing** 22, the Inner Chapters and **Huang-t'ing Wai-ch'ing** the Outer Chapters of the Gold Pavilion

***hun*** 128, 129, 135, 136, 170, the yang aspects of spirit, soul, as opposed to *po* (*p'o*) the physical and emotional aspects

***hundun*** (huntun) 69, 117, 118, 129, 130, 137, 145, 175, a term used by Chuang-tzu and later Taoist masters for primordial chaos, the demiurge, T'ai-chi (Taiji) and its personification as seen in chapter 7 of the Chuang-tzu

***hungtou*** (hung-t'ou) 8, a Redhat popular healer; see ***fashi***, ***Hoatsu***
***huntun*** see ***hundun***

# I

***I Ching*** (*Yijing*) 3–4, passim, the classic Book of Changes
**Illuminative Way** 162, one of the four stages of mystic prayer, namely, Purgative, Illuminative, Dark Night (apophasis, kenosis) and Unitive

# J

**Jade Chamber** 107, another term for the Gold Pavilion
**Jade Flower** 143, 147, 149, drop of yin born in the depths of yang fire; the trigram *li* purified by Taoist meditation in the Gold Pavilion
**Jade Ladies** 117, 121, 125, six Taoist spirits who protect the meditator from sullying thoughts and desires
**Jade Mushroom** 149, drop of yang born in the depths of yin; the trigram *kan* purified by Taoist meditation in the Gold Pavilion
**Jade Pavilion** 113, another term for the Gold Pavilion
**jade pool** 99, 101, 102, 103, 131, a term for the kidneys, as used in the Gold Pavilion text
**jade tree** 107, the sinews of primordial breath passing through the veins and arteries to renew the body
***jen*** (ren) 112, 114, 115, 124, 127, 129, the channel for conducting qi breath from the nose down the front of the body to the base of the spine during meditation
**Jenghe** 163, Amdo dialect for a Tantric Idam protective spirit
***jia*** 175, one of six protective spirits of Taoist meditation
***jiao*** (chiao) 8, 169, **Jiao** (Chiao) **Festival** 14, Taoist rites of village or temple renewal
***jing*** 75, passim, essence, the power of intuition, centered in the belly (*xia dantian*); also, essence, semen
***Jing gui shen er yuan ji*** "respect the spirits and demons, keep distant," a phrase from the Analects of Confucius
***ju*** (*ru*) 122, the yin entrance to the Gold Pavilion; see **ch'u**

*Glossary and Index of Special Terms*

## K

**k'an** (*kan*) 119, 121, passim, the trigram that represents water; see **li**

**Kangba** the people of Kang, East Tibet; includes west Szechuan, northeast Tibet, southeast Qinghai, north Yunnan

**kataphatic** 9, 11, prayer of visualization and imagination; the possessed medium trance, shaman vision journey

**kataphatic symbols** 75

**kenosis** xii, 154, 155, 156, 157, 162, self-emptying, prayer of,

**kenotic** 11, 68, 158, empty, "Dark Night" of the soul and senses in prayer

**Kuanyin** (Guanyin, Jpn., Kannon) 160, 161, 178, Chinese name for the Sanskrit Avalokitesvara, Bodhisattva of Compassion

**kuan-yüan** 100, passim, entrance to the Gold Pavilion; midway between the fifth lumbar vertebrae on the back and the navel

**k'un** (*kun*) 113, 114, 118, 121, passim, the trigram that stands for pure yin, opposite of *ch'ien*, for pure yang

**kung fu** (*gongfu*) 17, 123, a term used in English to represent various kinds of martial arts; in Taoist usage, it refers to any kind of interior practice, self-perfection

**Kung-tzu** 108, Confucius

## L

**Labrang temple** xiv, 162, 163, the great Gelugpa monastery of Eastern Amdo province, Tibet; now in southern Gansu, on the border of Qinghai

**Lao-tzu** (Laozi) 7, passim, the legendary founder of religious/philosphical Taoism, author of the *Tao-te Ching*

**Laozi** 14, Lao-tzu

**li** 42, a Chinese measure for spatial distance (about ½ kilometer)

**li** 169, 170, the Chinese term for ritual, offering, courtesy, sacrifice

**li** 119, 121, passim, the trigram that depicts fire

**Liji** 170, early Han dynasty (206 B.C.E - 25 C.E.) Ritual Classic; the *Yüeh-ling* Chapter was used to formulate Taoist ritual meditation

**ling** 113, 170, a term for spiritual power, insight

193

**Lingbao** (Ling-pao) Taoism 22, one of the three early religious Taoist schools

**Ling-pao Chen-wen** 125, the Lingbao True Writs, ritual meditations for harmony between the inner organs of the body and nature

**Lingbao Wufu** 76, five talismans used in Taoist ritual to establish harmony between the body and nature

*lingdao* 52, 54, a term used in modern China for a boss or leader

*ling-pao* see **Lingbao**

*ling-t'ai* (*lingtai*) 107, 108, passim, a Taoist term for the heart

*liu-chia* (*liujia*) 180, six terrifying Taoist protective spirits

*liu-fu* 115, 141, the six lower organs of the peritoneal region of the body

*liu-ting* (*liuding*) 180, six peaceful Taoist protective spirits

**Lotus World mandala** 157, 159, one of the two great meditative mandala of Tantric Buddhism; see **Vajra Dhatu**

**lower cinnabar field** 32, 79, 86, 177; see *xia dantian*

*lu* 7, 9, 141, 171, a register or list of spirits' names, summons, and visual appearance given to a Taoist at the time of initiation; the equivalent of Abhiseka (Guanding) in Tantric Buddhist practice

**Lugu Lake** 181, home of the matriarchal Muosuo people; see **Daba** rites

**Lunghu Shan** 21, Dragon-Tiger Mountain, home of the Celestial Master or Zhengyi school of Taoism

# M

**Madhyamika** (Chn. Sanlun, Zhonglun) 177, the Buddhist way of apophatic or emptying, non-judgmental prayer

**Mahakala** (Tbt. Gurkor) 163, 182, male figure of a violent Idam protective deity

**Mahakali** (Tbt. Dzamenje) 160, 163, 182, female form of an Idam protective deity

**Mahayana** 96, 180, The Great Vehicle, salvation oriented Buddhism popular in East and Southeast Asia

**Maitreya** (Chn. Milo, Jpn. Miroku) 160, Bodhisattva of the future

**Mao Shan** ix, 95, 102, 125, 143, 151, 173, home of the Highest Pure Taoist meditation school

**middle or center cinnabar field** 177, see *zhong dantian*

## Glossary and Index of Special Terms

**mi-chueh** (*mijue*) 25, 173, directions for Taoist and Tantric meditation learned by oral transmission from master to disciple

**mingmen** (*ming-men*) 100, 135, 139, 142, 147, the fifth lumber vertebrae in the meditation tradition; male organ in the sexual hygiene tradition

**ming-t'ang** (*mingtang*) 108, 109, 132, 135, 136, 138, 143, 144, "bright palace" Taoist meditative term for the heart

**Mount K'un-lun** 109, 111, 127, 128, Taoist term for the upper cinnabar field, i.e., the pineal gland in the brain

**mudra** (Chn. shouyin) 154, 176, 178, hand symbols used as talismanic signs to summon spirits during meditation

**Muosuo** 172, 181, matriarchal people on the border of Yunnan-Szechuan-Tibet, who preserve the Bon rites of Tibet

## N

**Naxi** (Nakhi) 172, people of the Lijiang district in Yunnan who preserve the Bon rituals of Tibet (see **Dongba**)

**neitan** (*neidan*) 124, the meditations of internal alchemy

**Ngapa** 172, Tibetan priests of Amdo (Qinghai, northeast Tibet) whose rites, exorcisms, and paraphernalia are similar to Redhat Taoist usage

**ni** 132, to go backward, i.e., to return from the many to the one, trace backward through the process of nature to the Tao of origin

**nien** 145, to be one with the Tao through the year long changes in nature

**ning** 49, a term used by Chuang-tzu to express non-change, i.e., one with the eternal Tao

**nonbeing** 29, 146, (Chn. *wu*), the word used to describe the Tao, when *yu*, to have being or existence, is used to describe nature

**North Pole** (Chn. Beiji) **Taoism** 22, meditation based on the North Pole star, focusing on Tao as center of the cosmos (see **Peichi**)

**North Star** (Beidou, Pei-tou) 121, the seven stars of the Big Dipper which always point to the north pole

## P

**Peichi** (Beiji) 130, the North Pole star, focal point of the northern heavens.

**pi** (*bi*) 130, a circular jade ornament with a hollow center; symbol for yin

**p'in** (*pin*) 102, 130, female, symbol of yin, Tao as mother

**p'o** (*po*) 128, 129, 135, 136, 170, the yin or bodily aspects of the soul-spirit. There are three *hun* and seven *p'o* aspects of soul

**polestar** 119, 130, 131, see **North Star, Peichi**

**posterior heavens** (*hou-t'ien, houtian*) 103, 125, the world of change in nature; see ***yu-wei chih tao*, Tai-chi, te** (*de*) opposite is the prior heavens

**primordial breath** (Chn. *yüan-ch'i, yuanqi*) 72, passim, the qi or energy gestated by the eternal Tao

**Primordial Heavenly Worthy** (Yüan-shih T'ien-tsun) 108, Tao as gestating

**prior heavens** (*hsien-t'ian, xiantian*) 133, 134, the abode of the eternal unchanging Tao (*wu-wei chih Tao*, wuchi)

**pu-hsiang** (*buxiang*) 145, not fortuitious, unfortunate, unlucky

**Pure Land Buddhist** 154, 180, belief that salvation or the "Pure Land" is won by invoking the name of Amida

## Q

**qi** (*ch'i*) 7, 17, passim, breathing in and out, as distinguished from **yuanqi** (*yüan-ch'i*) existence as energy generated from the transcendent Tao

**qi breath**, 17, 18, 31–32, passim, **qi** can be defined as primal energy (**yuanqi**) or breathing in and out, visualizing breath to enter the blood system and circulate through the body

**qigong** (*ch'i-kung*) **meditation** 17, 123, 179, meditating on the flow of qi through the body; visualizing qi energy coming in and going out from the body

**Qingwei** (Ch'ing-wei) "Pure Refined" Taoism 22, 173, the use of siddham Sanskrit mantra and mudra to visualize thunder and lightning, purify the body

# Glossary and Index of Special Terms

**Quanzhen** (Ch'uan-chen) "All True" Taoism 15, 23, 173, reformed Taoism, late Sung dynasty and thereafter

## R

**Redhat** (Hung-t'ou) Taoists 8, 9, 11, 23, 172, 173, popular Taoism, healers, exorcists of southeast China; rituals are similar to Bon, Dongba, and Amdo Ngapa (Ngawa) priests

**Rekong** 182, (Chn., Tongren), a town in Qinghai province famous for Tanka Tibetan Buddhist paintings

*ren* (*jen*) channel 82, 112, the visualization of breath flowing down the front of the body to the base of the spine

**Rongwo temple** 182, a Gelugpa temple of Rekong, Qinghai, Northeast Tibet

## S

*saigong* 9, Minnan/Taiwanese dialect for a Taoist

**Samatha-vipasyana** 154, 176, sanskrit term for cessation and contemplation, literally "stop" (mental images) and "look" (contemplate), an early form of Ch'an (Zen) practiced in China

*san-chiao* (*sanjiao*) 1, 74, 135, 136, 139, 140, 150, the "triple warmers," acupuncture point on the spine; three passages which "warm" (nourish) the body (food, liquid, breath)

**San-ch'ing** (Sanqing) 108, passim, the Three Pure Ones, the trinity of Taoist spirits who gestate, mediate, and indwell in the macro and microcosm

*shang dantian* (*shang tan-t'ien*) 78, 79, 144, the upper cinnabar field, the pineal gland in the head

**Shangqing** (Shang-ch'ing) Taoism 25, 102, 125, 173, the teachers of the Gold Pavilion meditation tradition; see **Mao Shan**

**Shao Hao** (Shao-hao) 14, 109, spirit patron of the west, autumn, lungs

*she* **spirit** 174, the spirit of the soil and crops in Chuang-tzu

*shen* 49, 80, 170, passim, spirit, soul; located in the heart, shen as will governs all the spiritual powers of the body

*shen-ming* 114, "bright spirits," spiritual forces of the body and nature visualized as separate entities

**Shen Nung** (Shen Nong) 13, 109, spirit patron of the south, summer, heart

*shih* 124, a period of 120 minutes, measure of time spent in meditation. A 40-minute period in quiet repose is considered minimal

**sit in forgetfulness** see **zuowang**

**six *ting* ladies** 113, 114, 115, protective spirits of Taoist ritual meditation

*sunya* (Chn., *kong*, *xu*) the Sanskrit term for emptiness

# T

**T'ai-chi** (*taiji*) 29, 63, 68, 103, 118, 175, 176, Great Origin, Tao of immanence, mother Tao as gestating qi

**tai chi chuan** (*taijiquan*) 17, 18, 83, 123, graceful exercises following qi's flow in the body

*t'ai-hsüan* (*taixuan*) 147, 148, the source of qi breath, Tao in the center

*taiji* see **T'ai-chi**

*t'ai-yin* (*taiyin*) 146, the Great Yin, the great ocean, source of the drop of yang that renews the cosmos

*t'ai-yüan* (*taiyuan*) 148, the kidneys

**tanka** xii, 160, 161, 163, 165, 177, 182, Tibetan paintings depicting the visualizations of Tantric meditation

**Tantric** xi, 96, 153–154, passim, meditation practice that uses the entire person, body (mudra), mouth (mantra) and mind (mandala) to pray

**Tantric Buddhism** 15, 22, 153, passim, Tantric practice, as found in Tibet, parts of Japan, and to a lesser extent in China

*Tao-ch'ang* (*Daochang*, Jp., Dojo) x, 158, a place for meditation or ritual practice; "Tao" is present

**Taoist** (Daoshi) 11, passim, a person who has received a *lu* register that includes instructions for ritual, qi meditation, mudra, dance, music and healing

**Tao of Transcendent Act** (*wuwei chih Tao*) 103, the *wuwei* act of Tao which gestates qi primordial breath; see **transcendent Tao**

*Tao-te Ching* (*Daode Jing*) 3–4, passim, the five-thousand word,

# Glossary and Index of Special Terms

eighty-one chapter book attributed to Lao-tzu

**te** (de) 3, 58, 117, passim, the visible, moving aspects of Tao in nature

**Theravada** 96, the Buddhism of south and southeast Asia, emphasizing the self-perfection of the practitioner

**the Three Teachings** 1, Confucianism for human relationships, Buddhism for the afterlife, and Taoism for harmony between the body and nature

**t'ien-ken** (*tiangen*) 132, 149, acupuncture point on the head used as a reference for qi meditation

**t'ien-men** (*tianmen*) 140, the trigram qian, the northwest direction

**Transcendent Act** 29, 118, wu-wei, the work of the Tao gestating qi in nature

**transcendent being** 28, an entity of which the notion "being" cannot be predicated, i.e., *wu-wei chih tao*

**transcendent Tao** 6, 12, 34, 43, 167, the Tao named as Wu, as distinct from the immanent Tao when named *yu*, or T'ai-chi, Tao as gestating mother

**true person** see ***zhenren*** (*chen-jen*) a person who is one with Tao

**tsang** see ***zang***

**ts'un** (*cun*) 101, to meditate; also, an inch, i.e., the drop of yang qi gestated by Tao in the depths of the yin ocean

**ts'un t'ien** (*cun tian*) 112, a technical term for the meditation in which east's wood and south's fire are alchemically refined into a drop of qi

**tsuo-wang** see ***zuowang***

**tu** (*du*) 112, 114, 115, 124, 127, 129, the visualized channel for circulating breath from the base of the spine upward, over the top of the head to the mouth

**tzu-jan** (*ziran*) 117, 128, nature, natural

## V

**Vairocana** 159, 160, the Buddha seen as bright as the sun, in Tantric practice

**Vaisravana** 159, the Buddhist protective spirit of the north

**Vajra Dhatu** (Vajradhatu) 158, the Vajra World mandala

**Virudhaka** 159, the Buddhist protective spirit of the south

**Virupaksa** 159, the Buddhist protective spirit of the west

# W

*wei dao ji xu* 89, "only Tao dwells in the void," a phrase from chapter four of the Chuang-tzu

**Wei Huacun** (Wei Hua-ts'un) ix, 6, 14, 22, 25, 69, 102, 123, 125, 143, 165, 171, 173, first recognized woman Taoist master d. 334 C.E.; transmitted the *Gold Pavilion* classic

*weilü* 111, 132, 149, acupuncture point used as a place of focus during meditation

*wu* 28, 117, 118, not, non-being, non-moved first mover's action

*wuchi* (*wuji*) 103, the transcendent source, the Tao of wu-wei, as opposed to *T'ai-chi* (Taiji) or *te* (de) the immanent, visible Tao

**Wudang Shan** xiv, 22, the home of Taoist martial arts, Polestar school

*wu-ku* (*wugu*) 142, the five grains, starches to be avoided in the ideal diet

*wu-t'ou* (*wutou*) 8, Blackhat Taoists, who belong to the Dragon-Tiger Taoist school and know the rites of the "Yellow" register for burial

*wu-tsang* (*wu zang*) 115, the five "storage" organs of the body: liver, heart, lungs, kidneys, spleen

*wuwei* (*wuwei*) 29, 39, 44, 119, 137, transcendent or "non" act, the gestation of primordial qi from Tao

*wuwei chih tao* (wuwei zhi dao) 12, 68, 103, 125, passim, the ultimate transcendent Tao gestating primordial qi

*wu yong* 57, a term used by Chuang-tzu as a pun to describe the person who is "one with Tao:" i.e., "no" use means "Tao" can dwell within, as in the case of the great gnarled tree left uncut by carpenters

# X

*xia* (*hsia*) 175, the lowest place, where the Lao-tzu points out, water always flows. "The Ocean is the greatest of all creatures because it likes to be in the lowest place."

# Glossary and Index of Special Terms

**xia dantian** (*hsia tan-t'ian*) 32, 78, 79, 86, 100, 102, 103, 158, the lower cinnabar field, the centering place in the body just below the navel used as a focal point in meditation

**xinzhai** (*hsin-chai*) 24, 25, 52, 53, 89, 110, 171, 174, heart-fasting, abstaining from judgmental thought and selfish desires

**xukong** (*hsü-k'ung*) emptiness, kenosis, apophasis; the mind and heart are "emptied" during meditation

## Y

**yang** passim, the male, bright, active principle of change in nature

**yi** 169, 170, change, i.e., the cyclical changes that occur regularly in nature

**Yijing** (*I Ching*) 4, passim, the ancient Book of Changes, a classic in the Taoist and Confucian tradition

**yin** passim, the female, hidden, receptive principle of nature

**yin-yang five phase system** 4, passim, the time-honored cosmological system of China; also called five elements, five movers, five principles

**yin-yang philosophy** 3–4, 16, passim, the archetypal structured cosmology of ancient China

**yinyang wuxing** (*yin-yang wu-hsing*) 4, the yin-yang five phase system

**yu** (*you*) 28, the immanent, moving Tao of nature, as opposed to *wu* the constant unchanging Tao of wu-wei

**Yü** (as in Yü Pu) 150, Yü the Great, a mythical king who stopped the floods by pacing sacred dance steps, called *Yü Pu* the dance of Yü, based on the magic square of nine:

    4  9  2
    3  5  7
    8  1  6

**yüan** 131, passim, primordial, origin

**yüan-ch'i** 31, see **yuanqi**

**yuanqi** (*yüan-ch'i*) 31, 127, 145, primordial breath

**Yüan-shih T'ien-tsun** 108, Primordial Heavenly Worthy, Tao as gestating qi

***yu-chüeh*** 99, 100, 102, acupuncture point just below the navel, used as a reference in meditation

***yung*** 124, a variant term for the *ren* passage from the nose down the front of the body to the base of the spine, during meditation

***yü-nü*** 118, jade women, Taoist protective spirits who guard the mind and heart from distraction

***yü-shen*** (*yü-chen*) 111, 132, 149, acupuncture point on the back of the skull used as a reference point during meditation

***yü-wei chih tao*** (*yuwei zhi dao*) 118, 175, the Tao of change in nature

# Z

***zang*** (*tsang*) 73, 177, one of the five main organs of the body; see ***wu-tsang***

***zhenren*** (*chen-jen*) 60–62, Tao-realized person; a person who is one with Tao

***zhi*** 52, the will

***zhong dantian*** 79, 124, the middle cinnabar field

***zui taiping*** 175, drunk on peace

***zuowang*** (*tsuo-wang*) 24, 25, 64, 89, 110, 171, 174, the meditation of Chuang-tzu for "sitting in forgetfulness," emptying the mind

# Bibliography and Further Readings

———, *Huang-t'ing Ching* (*Huangting Jing*), *Yunjiqiqian,* (The *Gold Pavilion* classic), Beijing, Baiyunguan edition, 1435.

Anderson, P., *The Method of Holding the Three Ones; A Taoist Manual of Meditation,* London: Curzon Press, 1980.

Boltz, Judith, *A Survey of Taoist Literature,* Berkeley, California: Institute of East Asian Studies, University of California, Berkeley, Center for Chinese Studies, 1987.

Huang, J. and M. Wurmbrand, *The Primordial Breath,* Torrance, California: Original Books, 1987.

Kohn, Livia, *Early Chinese Mysticism,* Princeton, New Jersey: Princeton University Press, 1992.

Lagerwey, J., *Taoist Ritual in Chinese Society,* New York: 1987.

Liu, I-ming, *Huang-t'ing Ching Chieh* (commentary on the *Huangting Jing*), Jiyunguan edition, 1799.

Maspero, H., *Taoism and Chinese Religion,* Amherst, Massachusetts: University of Massachusetts Press, 1981.

Robinet, I., *Taoist Meditations,* Albany: State University of New York at Albany, 1993.

Saso, Michael, *Taoism and the Rite of Cosmic Renewal*, Pullman, Washington: Washington State University Press, 1990.

———, *The Teachings of Taoist Master Chuang*, New Haven, Connecticut: Yale University Press, 1978.

———, *Blue Dragon, White Tiger*, Honolulu: University of Hawaii Press, 1990.

———, *Tantric Art and Meditation*, Honolulu: University of Hawaii Press, 1990.

———, *A Taoist Cookbook*, Boston: Charles E. Tuttle Company, Inc., 1994.

Schipper, K. M., *Concordance du Huang-t'ing Ching; Nie-King et Wai-King* Paris: Ecôle Francaise d'extrème Orient, 1975.

———, *Le corps Taoiste; Corps Physique, Corps Social*, Paris: Fayard, 1982.

Strickmann, M., *Le taoism du Mao chan; chronique d'une revelation* Paris: College de France, Institut des Hautes Etudes Chinoises: Presses Universitaire de France, 1981.

Welch, H. and Seidel, A., *Facts of Taoism*, New Haven, Connecticut: Yale University Press, 1979.